CALLED TO SERVE
A PRACTICAL HANDBOOK FOR PASTORS

CALLED TO SERVE

A PRACTICAL HANDBOOK FOR PASTORS

G. H. Grose
E. F. Grose

ISPCK
1997

Called to Serve—A Practical Handbook for Pastors—Published by the Indian Society for Promoting Christian Knowledge (ISPCK), Post Box 1585, Kashmere Gate, Delhi–110006, under the Indian Contextual Theological Education Series–2

First Edition 1993
Reprinted 1997

Price: Rs. 50.00

ISBN: 81-7214-146-7

CONTENTS

FOREWORD

With the phenomenal rise in population and rapid growth in numbers in our cities, towns and villages, pastors today face a situation which makes heavy demands on their physical, spiritual and mental resources.

Most congregations look up to their pastor. He is required to be a sympathetic and understanding counsellor, a caring visitor, a persuasive preacher of God's word, an able organiser of the day to day life of his pastorate, an enabler and builder of leadership among the children, youth as well as men and women.

To meet the expectations of his people and also to fulfil his own calling as a diligent minister of Christ he needs to accept a self-imposed discipline which includes personal prayer, study of the Bible as well as other relevant reading material and to plan and apportion the time he has at his disposal.

I am very pleased that 'The Book for Pastors' so wisely, ably and often humorously covers the important areas of the pastor's life and work. It provides practical suggestions and advice so that he can grow spiritually and thus become an effective minister of Christ's Gospel.

What Rev. Geoffery and Mrs. Elsie Grose together, as a husband and wife team, have so generously and yet so humbly shared with us is their most valuable experience gathered over a remarkably blessed ministry of over forty years in both rural and urban India. A considerable part of their ministry was spent in Free Church, Green Park, New Delhi. I was the Bishop of Delhi Diocese at that time and I know how much both of them were loved by their congregation and that at least four young men were inspired by them to enter the full time ministry of the Church of North India. What they have to communicate is most up-to-date and relevant to the present day needs and challenges which pastors of all church traditions are likely to face in their congregations today.

Pastoralia is taught in theological colleges by and large as a theoretical subject and much of what is taught needs practical application which can only be gained through experience. The significance of this book lies precisely in the experience gained and shared by Rev. and Mrs. Grose in their long ministry.

Young and newly ordained pastors will benefit much from this book. So also older pastors who still want to learn and re-examine their pastoral approach and wish to enhance the effectiveness of their ministry. I have learnt much from this book myself. The mature advice shared in it will prove beneficial and I have much satisfaction in commending it to all pastors. They will find it an excellent reference book for their pastoral work.

Dalhousie, H.P.   Bishop Maqbul Caleb
March, 1993

ABOUT THE AUTHORS

Rev. Geoffrey Grose and his wife, Elsie worked in India from 1953 to 1988. After serving with the Baptist Union of North India in Bihar and U.P. in district work, they moved to New Delhi in 1962. There they served as pastor and wife in the Parliament Street Free Church, and then in the Green Park Free Church. In 1970 Rev. Grose became a Presbyter in the newly formed Church of North India. They have three children, all born in India. Now retired and living in the U.K. they retain a great love for India and its people.

-o-o-o-

DEDICATION

With gratitude to God, this book is dedicated to all who contributed so lovingly and patiently to the authors understanding of the pastoral ministry.

-o-o-o-

ACKNOWLEDGMENTS

A number of people have encouraged us in the writing of this book. Especially we must thank the Rt. Revd. Maqbul Caleb for agreeing to provide the Foreword. Mrs. Valerie Adams introduced us to using a computer and kindly allowed us the use of her own machine. The Revd. E. Leslie Wenger gave time to reading through the manuscript and correcting errors, and made many valuable suggestions, most of which have been incorporated into the book.

INTRODUCTION

This is a book about the work of a pastor and his wife, and comes out of years of experience in Church work in India. My wife and I are now retired, so to share some of our experience with fellow pastors will be an extension to our ministry.

From our days of training for the ministry we have been involved in Church work. The healthiness of Church life and the outreach of the Church into the world is our interest. This does not mean that we regard other occupations as second-class or optional. Rather we see all such activities as part of the Church's life. Medicine and Education, Farming, Business, Social projects and Counselling, and any other activity to which Christians are directed by God are all aspects of the Church in action.

Nevertheless, we regard the pastoral ministry as having a unique function, for whatever a Christian's occupation or profession, she or he needs to be spiritually alert, and it is the pastor's task to provide the needed guidance, wisdom, fellowship, encouragement and a true understanding of the Bible.

A group of people were once asked to write out a job-description for a pastor. One job-description took nine typed pages! Another read something like this: "A pastor's job is to faithfully read aloud the service of the Church day by day without changing so much as a word." That this is not a satisfactory job-description will become clear in the pages ahead.

Both my wife and I come from a Baptist background. Both of us had secular jobs before offering for full-time service and studying in theological colleges. From 1953 to 1963 we worked in Indian towns and villages in a supportive and sometimes supervisory role. Then followed twenty five years in the pastoral ministry in a city Church.

We view the local church as the people of God gathered in one place and priesthood as a matter of service rather than status. The gifts God gives are widely distributed among His people, and must be respected. These gifts are not centered wholly or primarily in the clergy, though God used his ministers as leaders and under-shepherds.

It should be mentioned that in the following chapters personal details do not refer to any of our colleagues or fellow church members, past or present.

We realise that many pastors reading this book will feel their situation is entirely different to anything mentioned. Yet, even if a few ideas can be seen as helpful, this book will have served its purpose.

Although this book has been written jointly, for ease of reading we have used the first person singular throughout.

The Pastor and the Church

"Visit Aurobindo Place – near the church in Hauz Khas". I was interested to read this advertisement on the back of a Delhi Transport Bus, because it referred to the church where I lived and served. The reference was, of course, to the church building, which is one of the ways in which we use the word 'church' but the same word may be used to describe a local group of Christians or to refer to Christians everywhere, the Church in the world. Until the third century A.D. there is no record of specific church buildings. The early Christian community met in homes. The Jews had their synagogues and it would be natural for Christians to follow this pattern of a building set aside for worship, teaching and fellowship. Every permanent congregation I have known has desired to have its own building, and whether the structure be an architectural masterpiece or the simplest construction of thatch and bamboo, such buildings have become hallowed places where God's people meet with their Lord and with each other. In matters of spiritual priority, church buildings may be far down the list, yet Jesus called the temple in Jerusalem 'My Father's House' and 'a house of prayer for all nations'. So, if we are fortunate enough to have a building, let us be thankful and take care of its upkeep and appearance, with its doors open to all who come seeking fellowship.

The Church is sometimes called 'The Bride of Christ' and sometimes 'The Body of Christ'. Both these terms convey the notion of the Church being alive. A bride is a person anxious to look her best and to be her best for her partner. 'The Body of Christ' conveys the sense of a living entity, feet, hands and mouth, all controlled by the head, which is Christ. This would be a description of the whole Church on earth and in heaven, but it is difficult to visualise the Church in her totality, except in a visionary way as in the Book of Revelation. For most of us 'Church' means a large denomination, with the Church being all these denominational Churches, including Orthodox, Roman and Pentecostal, etc., viewed together. Even so, in whatever way the Churches (capital C) or local churches (small c) are active, – in worship, ritual, service to the distressed, prayer, – to be true activities of The Church, these activities must be linked to the head, Christ Jesus. No prayer has any spiritual value unless God is inspiring it and hearing it. No sacrament consists merely of ritualistic movements and incantations. A sacrament is surely an act through which Christ communicates Himself to people and people lay themselves open to God's inspiration and assurance. As pastors, much of our thinking is related to Sunday services and ancillary meetings. We need to remind ourselves constantly that our work in the churches is part of a larger work in which God is extending His kingdom and preparing the whole Church (and helping people prepare each other) as the Bride of Christ. In this way the Church, seven days a week and twenty-four hours a day, is the Body of Christ, diffused throughout society. It is a host of people inspired by God to be channels for the input of His will into world affairs; an extension, though we have to say it with awe and humility, of the Incarnation. God's act of redemption was complete in Jesus Christ's first advent, but has to be applied in every new generation. So God's redemptive work is continuing. Work worthily done for God demonstrates His spiritual presence. But where the churches fail to mirror God's will in daily living, there the Church is failing to be the Body of Christ.

So we move to the third use of the word 'church'; a local community of Christians organised for worship and service and usually meeting regularly in a building set aside for this purpose. A very important aspect of the life of such a church is the fellowship members have with each other. My pastoral experience began in a Union church. The congregation was drawn from many traditions, Syrian, Anglican and Basel Mission, Methodist and Baptist, etc. but functioned as a unity for worship, sacraments, fellowship and outreach. Coming from Baptist Church background, this was a wonderful learning experience, a taste of the wider Church in a local setting. While admitting weaknesses, the church managed its own affairs with quite a degree of success. In 1970, after the inauguration of the Church of North India, this church joined the uniting Church, and I with presbyters from other denominations, became part of the unified ministry.

Being part of a much larger organization, and adapting to the necessary give and take of sharing different traditions, brought many new experiences. For example, I experienced the discipline of serving under a bishop. Something of what this meant was brought home to me months later. Continuing with the usual practice of preparing candidates for Church Membership and receiving them into membership at a regular church service, I found I was unwittingly acting contrary to episcopal tradition by not inviting the bishop to conduct the confirmation service and give his blessing to the new members. This was one of many instances where different church traditions had to be dovetailed into each other. But even such difficulties were used by the Holy Spirit to help us discover our true basis for unity, and the process brought with it a great sense of fellowship.

One of the challenges that pastors face is that of building up a sense of caring fellowship on a local church level. The larger the church, the more difficult the problem, for there are groupings that spontaneously occur and it takes a real act of human will plus some divine prompting to help groups realise that they do belong together and have a responsibility for each other. In small churches also the same problem arises because local memories last a long time and divisions within families are not easily healed. A pastor must be alert to the danger of appearing to favour one group or clique within his congregation, yet at the same time seek to draw his people together across the boundaries of family divisions, ethnic loyalties or habit. Frankly, people find it hard to accept correction by the pastor, but may well be open to ideas that come through reading scripture. So any encouragement a pastor can give to systematic Bible reading will bring a blessing. Other ways in which the fellowship of the church can be strengthened are dealt with in following chapters.

There are times when a pastor feels that he is 'doing it all himself' and he gets frustrated. There was one occasion in our church when we were to be visited by a V.I.P. from overseas. In order to make his time with us more interesting, we decided to invite him to share a meal with us and meet representatives of those who were serving in the church. So we made our list of invitees. Members of the church committee would be there, plus the Sunday School Superintendent, the Youth Fellowship leaders, someone from the Fabric Committee, the president of the Women's Fellowship, the church librarian, the Bible Readings secretary, the man who looked after the fund for helping children of leprosy patients and the lady who similarly served a Home for the elderly, the church organist and choir leader. . . The list grew longer and longer until we wondered however we would fit everybody into our small apartment.

But I must confess to my own astonishment and shame that I had never really given thought to just how many people there were quietly serving in so many different ways. They themselves were pleasantly surprised to meet many others who were helping in the church. If you take time to list all the people in your congregation who are, however small the task, serving the church in some way, you will probably be surprised to find how long the list is. And you don't need to wait for a visiting V.I.P. to have a fellowship meal together!

Chapter

2

Called to Serve

"In India there is no such thing as a call to God's service." This remark, made to me by an Indian colleague in the ministry, surprised me immensely. My own call to ministry in the Church had been so definite and my fellow-students and tutors at theological college had all shared such a sense of calling, that I had assumed it was an experience common to all in the pastoral ministry. Perhaps my friend wanted me to understand that some become pastors in the same way that others become civil servants or nurses. They have a sense of a job to be done to which they can bring Christian integrity and intellectual ability. It is a way of earning a living which is open to them through circumstances rather than through a divine call.

What, then, do I mean by 'call'? This can best be explained by describing my own experience, though God may work differently for different people. My sense of call began to develop during military service in the 1939-45 war. I was posted to various parts of the world, including Japan, and met many people. In this way I was given an understanding of the world-wide Church and some of its needs. By the time I was demobilised, I had a feeling that God had His purpose in giving me these wartime experiences, but as yet it did not amount to a definite call to the pastoral ministry. I shared my feelings with my pastor who encouraged me to serve in the church, and I became a leader of the Youth Fellowship. At this time I met and married my wife who was active in Sunday School and Youth work in her church and together we increasingly felt that the work we were doing was but a preliminary to something more. But what? Encouraged by my pastor, I took the Baptist Union's Home Preparation course for Lay Preachers and began to help in services in local churches. After months of living with this feeling of 'Something more', we attended a rally at which the speaker was a missionary – whose brother happened to have been my Sunday School teacher years earlier. The missionary and his wife invited any who might be interested in missionary service to speak with them after the service. With some hesitation, we shared with these friends what we had been feeling, we could think of many reasons that would make it impossible for us to become missionaries; we were already married and in those days it was almost unheard of for a married couple to be accepted for missionary service; we had no financial resources to pay for the necessary training; service in the army meant that I was older than usual for entering college. But the advice we received was "Take the first step, Make the offer. Keep praying – and if it is God's call, then He will certainly remove all the barriers." And that was what happened. There followed letters, interviews, advice, prayers, committees, all playing their part in confirming God's call into the ministry and to overseas service. For five or six years God had been nudging us toward this step and, having taken it, there came the inner assurance that this was indeed what God wanted.

As I write, I have before me the Order of Service of our Commissioning in 1953. In the synopsis it states "Elsie and Geoffrey will be working in co-operation with Indian and

European colleagues in the task of ministering to and increasing the Church in North India". We would not change a word of that, if we had to write it today.

So then, what can we say about this matter of calling. It is certainly a word found in the Bible. The Christians in Corinth were "called to be saints" (1 Cor 2:24) and this thought of all Christians being called can be found in several other of Paul's letters. However, John 20:21 speaks of the apostles being 'sent out' by Christ, and Acts speaks of Paul and Barnabas being 'set apart', so it would appear that within the general calling, is a specific calling to a particular office. Though it is not my intention to declare that no one can serve as a pastor without a definite sense of call, I can only affirm that I could not have undertaken the task myself, or continued through nearly 40 years, without the assurance that I was fulfilling the task to which God had called me.

A person in the diplomatic service of his country is 'authorised' to speak on behalf of the government of his country. In order to exercise that authority well, he must be in constant and close touch with his government and must curb his own aspirations where these do not properly represent those of the people who sent him. A pastor is appointed by God and draws the authority for his service from God. Without that sense of calling and appointment, and responsibility to God, the authority vested in the pastor can be a very dangerous thing. If I had to rely only on an appointment letter, I would feel my authorisation to be as flimsy as the paper it was written on. As it is, I can say "Lord, you sent me, please provide for me, guide me and use me."

'Call to ministry' does not necessarily mean 'Full-time service paid for by the Church'. A lay pastor or part-time pastor may have a call to the pastoral ministry. Also 'the call of God' can relate to other spheres of service. Especially when counselling young people seeking God's purpose for their lives, a pastor should have in mind the possibility of them serving God in a number of ways other than in the pastoral ministry.

How then does this sense of 'Being called' come about? The following outline of my own experience contains a number of strands, some though not necessarily all of which may be common to most people experiencing a call to the pastoral ministry.

i) I was brought up in a Christian home by parents who were good examples and who co-operated with and encouraged me.

ii) My wife's own sharing and encouraging helped the matter forward. For instance, she continued in employ-ment while I went to seminary.

iii) The sense of call went alongside a step by step response to events. For example, my wartime service introduced me to other Christian serving men and women as well as to fine men in the chaplaincy service. Through various postings, I gained a new world-outlook. On leaving the army, I received the encouragement of my pastor and took opportunities for Christian service as they came along, – youth work, lay preaching, etc. With the help of the same pastor, I began to study New Testament Greek, and another pastor later guided me through the process of entry into theological college. Responding to events in this way can be both a test that the call is genuine and also an indication of one's willingness to endure the discipline of study and preparation.

iv) Our church fellowships supported my wife and me in interest and prayer.

v) Time was a factor, for between the first sense of God's Call and completing training, seven years were to pass.

vi) Almost unnoticed, we were introduced into the system of checks and balances provided by Church committees at local, area, denominational and seminary level. Each of these helped vet 'the call'. The collective wisdom of the Church has a part to play in discerning the authenticity of an individual's sense of call.

vii) Finally, though perhaps this should be put first, the awareness throughout that God was overseeing the matter. It was seeking to know and fit in with His will that was our basic concern and we were aware of His confirmation and provision each step of the way. His provision included good health, companionship, finance, entry into theological college for myself and into missionary training college for my wife. Of course, through the years, finding God's will for our lives was a matter of earnest prayer, prayer that needs to go on as situations change and develop throughout the whole of life.

If the question should be asked, "Does one need God's call to be a pastor", I can only say that in the pastoral ministry there are times when loneliness has to be endured. Sometimes there is a great sense of failure and lack of fruitfulness. Difficulties arise which seem to threaten the stability of the church. There may be periods of poor health and times when one's good name and intentions are misrepresented. It is at such times that the assurance of God's calling gives the courage to keep going.

In conclusion, let me tell you a story. At the time of leaving seminary, the students of my year were invited to meet an Area Superintendent from the North of England. Many towns in the north are industrial and somewhat bleak. Also at that time. incomes of people living in the north tended to be lower than those in the south. The climate, too can be quite harsh in the north, with cold winds and early snow. The Superintendent put before the students who would shortly be seeking placements, the challenge of working in the north. With tongue in cheek he said, "It is amazing how many theological students are called to serve churches in the south!." How careful we must be that in responding to God's call we do not delude ourselves into choosing only those options where conditions are comfortable and easy.

The Pastor's Wife and Family

The story goes that a Roman Catholic clergyman, concerned about the ordination of women to the priesthood, gave this warning: "If this happens in our Church, at next year's Council the bishops will be coming with their wives – and the following year, bishops will be coming with their husbands!"

Some branches of the Church have already ordained women to the eucharistic ministry, but it is a fact that at the present time in India the majority of the clergy are male. This chapter, therefore, has in mind pastors who have wives and families. My wife and I had the awareness of being led together into the ministry of the Church, but we have known ministers' families where misunderstandings and incompatibilities have marred the pastor's ministry, and for this reason we have included this chapter.

Some pastors' wives are working women in their own right. Some have to take employment in order to bring in an income to help keep the family, – a sad reflection on the often inadequate scale of salary paid to pastors. Also a woman who has professional skills may feel quite unfulfilled by only routine home-duties. If it is decided that the wife should continue in employment after marriage, then it is for both husband and wife to carefully pray about and sort out such matters as: 'How will the work in the house be adequately done?', 'Is the wife to carry the full burden of maintaining a job and managing all the household duties?', 'What arrangements will be made for the care of the children?', 'How will the extra income be managed?', 'Does the wife's salary go into a joint bank account or does she retain control over it?'.

Unless questions of this nature are talked through and decisions made, they can be the cause of tensions and quarrels. Extra home responsibilities, such as taking children to and from school and supervising their homework, shopping etc., may be seen by church members as using time that the pastor ought to spend on church duties. Openness on such matters and frank discussion with the officers of the church will prevent misunderstandings. If it is possible for the wife to schedule her responsibilities so that she is seen to be taking part in the life of the church (perhaps helping with costumes for a Sunday School play, or sharing her experience as a Christian in a secular job with a Youth Fellowship discussion group) then some of the church members' fears relating to a pastor with a working wife will be allayed.

It has to be acknowledged that there are some wives, working or home-based, who do not want to assist in church related matters in any way. Such feelings may be based on a view of the church as a critical, unappreciative, unhelpful body of people. Sadly there may be some justification for such feelings, but total aloofness can be very unhelpful to the pastor whose work demands that he cares for all his flock. Resentment at some personal hurt suffered may underlie the wife's feelings, but with understanding and sympathy, may I suggest this attitude can be a failure to tread the way of the Cross? Of course, this is not always the reason why a wife does not take much part in the work of the church. Some women feel inadequate and unskilled while the church may have exaggerated expectations of the pastor's wife. Understanding and support from her husband will help her to discover her own talents and her part in the life of the church fellowship.

The pastor's wife often has to endure limitations that are peculiar to the manse; – loneliness when the husband has to be out on duty; a lack of freedom to pursue her own interests when the needs of the church always seem to have priority. She may get the impression that she is being treated like an unpaid servant of the church, getting no thanks and little respect. This is where a strong sense of partnership as husband and wife and as pastor and wife in the ministry of the Church is so important. A mutual sharing and obvious consideration for each other is needed. I say 'obvious consideration' because some pastors do love and respect their partners but forget to express that love and respect. This sense of partnership may develop during the years of ministry, but it is something to be considered when a marriage is being arranged.

The Church believes in theological training for its pastors, but it is still rare for a course of training to be offered to a minster's wife. Such training would be extremely helpful in preparing the wife for her role in the life of the church and in enabling her to understand and support her husband's ministry more effectively.

In our experience, the wife of a pastor has to walk a tightrope between involvement and exclusion. By this I mean that while the minister's wife can bring the blessing of her own personality and experience to such things as pastoral visiting, there are also times when she must accept that her presence may be interpreted as interference and unhelpful. While supporting and sharing with her husband wherever possible, she must also accept that the matters people share with her husband in confidence should not be divulged even to his wife! She is free to hold and express her own opinions, but needs to take care not to indulge in gossip or in making derogatory remarks about others. It has always seemed wise to us, that two members from one family should not serve on the Pastorate Committee of a church at the same time, and so we have adopted this as a policy for ourselves as well. This avoids the appearance of a wife being there solely to support her husband, or worse, embarrasing her husband by public disagreement! Disagreements there will be, of course, but they are best sorted out in the privacy of the home.

A few practical tips for the pastor's wife may be appropriate here. Embarrassment can be avoided, if one room in the manse is kept ready to receive visitors at any time. For us in our small apartment, this meant that my wife had to make space in the bedroom for her needlework, writing etc., leaving the living room reasonably tidy for the unexpected caller. A wife often has to drop what she is doing to receive visitors. To practise the art of welcoming people graciously rather than resenting the interruption not only makes the visitor feel at home but enables one to enjoy the visit. Having welcomed the caller, then how to deal with the question, 'May I see the pastor?'. Is the pastor to be interrupted in his study by every caller, or is it a matter that the wife can deal with herself, – a request to borrow the Christmas Father outfit, or to know the location of the next cottage meeting, – or does it require the listening ear of the pastor? Getting it right and treating all callers with respect so that no one goes away feeling offended is something the pastor's wife gradually learns from experience, and even then, sometimes makes mistakes.

There are the callers who come requesting money. We have found it helpful to follow the general rule that only the pastor gives money from the church funds. Callers in genuine need will be willing to call again when the pastor is available.

Dealing with criticism is more difficult than dealing with callers and it so often falls to the wife to do this. One's initial response is usually indignant self-defence. However it may be that there is some justification or some misunderstanding has caused the hurt, and to acknowledge this and apologise or to put right misunderstanding is not a sign of weakness but of strength. Should the criticism relate to her husband, then it is wisest for the wife not to get involved either in explanation or defence, but to refer the person directly to the pastor.

Children of the manse can be a real blessing, but how often more is expected of them than of other children! We've all heard, "Why should the pastor's children behave like that?". A pastor's children can suffer in two ways. Occasionally they are given preference not shown to other children, which makes them feel more important than they are, or they may have to fend for themselves while their parents are immersed in church business, and that can make them feel very neglected. It is dangerously easy for a pastor and wife to be very sensitive to the needs of the members of the church and remain unaware of the loneliness or neglect felt by their own children. When God gives children, He gives parental responsibilities with them. It is wrong to say, "I am doing the Lord's work, so He will look after my children." There may be times when this has to happen, but it should be the exception and not the rule. The rule is 'Let children know that they are wanted, loved and occupy a very special place in their parents' lives'.

Children are learning all the time, not just through instruction in schools, but by a process of absorption. What they see and hear in their homes is also part of their education. Many children of the manse, now adult, can look back and admit how much their lives were enriched through being part of the pastor's family. They have opportunity to meet many different people and their own attitudes to hospitality will have been received through their experience in the home. Allowing them to assist in small ways, – flowers for the tables, suggesting games for a children's party, answering the telephone (having been well taught to write down messages received) all helps the children to feel appreciated. It must always be remembered, however, that children cannot be expected to keep confidences, and it is only fair to them that nothing should be said in their presence which is of a confidential nature.

In the daily schedule of the Manse, make sure there is time for the children; time to read a story, time for a game and, as far as possible, time to have meals together. The meal table is the ideal place for sharing things that have happened and the latest 'in' jokes. Whenever possible, it is good for both parents to share prayer time with the children. We tend to think of bedtime as the time for prayer, but often the pastor is out on his round of pastoral visits or attending a committee meeting. Why not make the end of the evening meal, or the first meal of the day, the time for family devotions, when all the family are sitting together? Never forget that the pastor's children like any other children, look forward to outings and to an annual holiday. As you take care to relate properly to your own children, you will gain valuable understanding of how to relate to other children in the church.

While there are differences between town and village situations, in both cases people will look in to see what the pastor's family is doing. The pastor's house is a shop window for Christian home and family life. It has a great potential for witness.

As this book is written to share insights gained through my own experience in the ministry, I have not included a section dealing with the special needs of unmarried ministers. Most of what has been written will relate to all pastors, but there are undoubtedly special blessings and difficulties for the single minister. Some may feel that by remaining single they are able to give their undivided attention to the ministerial task.

However, they are also open to special temptations and need to show that they are maintaining a blameless life. All pastors feel the need to share their problems with someone who will understand and provide encouraging fellowship, and the single minister has to exercise great care and discernment in chosing those with whom he will share confidences. A colleague in the ministry may best meet this need and a caring bishop or district supervisor will have the needs of all his pastors in mind. The bond of fellowship within a fraternity of pastors gives encouragement and support to all the members, but perhaps specially to the single pastor.

Chapter

4

The Pastor's Personal Spirituality

Jesus reminded his followers that what comes out of the mouth, proceeds from the heart (Matt. 26:41). Ministry to the spiritual needs of others must always begin with preparing one's self. Here we will be considering the inner spiritual life of the pastor.

Near to where we live in England are chalky hills, and in these hills are springs of water that flow down the valleys to become larger rivers. The water that comes from the springs is pure and refreshing, but as the streams flow through farmland and industrial areas they are gradually polluted with farm and factory waste. The water is no longer fit for drinking but can cause illness. Similarly, in a pastor's life, as in the life of every Christian, the hidden springs have to be kept clean. No member of the clergy is free from the possibility of sin. Therefore how we keep our lives in good spiritual shape is of utmost importance for ourselves and for those to whom we minister.

One secret, which is an open secret, lies in the word 'Lord'. We often use the word, but it is worth asking whether we really mean it. "If I, then your Lord and Master. . ?" (John 13:13). Such a question looks for a response. See also Luke 6:46: "Why do you call me Lord?. . .", If He is Lord and Master, then **we** are disciples and servants. So is Jesus our Lord? Do we submit daily to the scrutiny of our lives by the Holy Spirit? It is all too easy to turn our consciences into 'our obedient servants', ready to provide us with excuses justifying our conduct or our attitudes. Therefore we need someone or something outside of ourselves to keep our consciences toned up. The reading of Scripture and prayer are two main sources of correction, but we also need to feed our minds with good books and to learn from the lives of good people around us.

During military service I learnt the importance of 'Part I Orders'. Details of the day's duties, changes of routine and possibilities of entertainments were posted outside the unit office each morning. Every man was expected to read the list daily, and woe betide the man who missed an appointment through failing to read the orders for the day. Ignorance was never accepted as a valid excuse! Another feature of military service was the daily inspection of quarters and kit. All had to be in good order and any shoddiness was quickly noted and brought its penalty. The spiritual life of a pastor can be likened to the life of a soldier in military service. We take our orders from our Lord through daily reading of scripture and through prayer as we acknowledge Him to be our Lord master. We keep our lives clean and open for inspection by the Holy Spirit through meditation on the written word and repentance.

A definite scheme of scripture reading with study notes provides a stimulus for thought, allows God to speak to us, and helps us avoid always turning to those passages that are most familiar and cease to challenge. There may be the odd occasion when, being extremely tired after a long journey or being unwell, the daily scripture study has to be missed. But while we depend on God's graciousness at all times and are thankful that we are not under 'law', still this must always be the exception and not the rule. A good rule is 'Bible before breakfast', and if we keep to this discipline, we will certainly know the benefit in our own lives and in our ministry All of us find time to wash, dress and eat before starting the day. Let it be just as much routine to take time for daily devotions. The pattern will not be the same for everyone. There are those who like to start the day with a walk in the fresh morning air, or some physical exercise. Many will want to start the day with an early morning cup of tea and a bath. All this helps to awaken the body and mind and can be a helpful preparation for the time of study and prayer, but it must be 'preparation for' and not 'in place of'.

I have mentioned study notes as an aid to studying scripture. Often the thoughts and comments which these contain are means by which God speaks. It is a sharing of wisdom and truth as God gives these to His people. Similarly, prayers written by others can help us in our own devotions. Usually we can express our personal thanks, confession and petition, but there are times when we feel dry or stale, or carelessly repetitive in our prayers, and it is at such times that a well-chosen anthology of prayers can help us express what we need to pray about.

My wife and I have always shared this early morning time of scripture reading and prayer together. Sometimes through one of us querying what the commentator says, or what the passage means, or the circumstances in which the scripture was written, new light is given to both of us. Also, it is our practice to pray aloud, turn by turn. Praying aloud has the advantage of keeping the thoughts focused and helps correct those periods of mind wandering from which we all suffer.

What about the content of this time of prayer? There are so many things to pray for, how do we remember them all and fit them into a reasonable time? Does our prayer sound like a tape-recording playing the same tune day after day? An aid to prayer that I have found useful over the years is in the shape of a postcard! This card (which can be used as a bookmark in the study notes) is divided into seven columns, one for each day of the week. Heading each day's column is Praise and Thanksgiving, with Confession and Repentance. Next come prayers for our immediate family members who are prayed for every day. After that each day is different. Close friends and relatives are shared between the days. Those with special needs, the elderly, orphaned children, the sick, people in demanding professions such as education, medicine, politicians and those in authority; each of these groups is remembered on a separate day. The Church and areas of outreach come next, then the local church and individuals with particular responsibilities. All this may sound very mechanical, but it was something recommended to me at a Youth Retreat many years ago, and as it has worked for me, I would recommend it to others.

MON	TUE	WED	THU	FRI	SAT	SUN
	P r a	i s e	a n d	T h a	n k s	
C o	n f e s	s i o n	a n d	Re pe	nt·a n c	e
		N ear	F a m	i l y		
AuntA	AuntB	UncleC	UncleD	Cousins	Cousins	Theo'l
Elderly	Orphans	Teachers	Medics	U.N.	Politicians	Seminaries
ChurchA	ChurchB	Radio	Bible Soc.	Publ'rs		Helpers
Friends,	ill	&	needy,	group	by	group

The list of people is constantly changing, so the card will need up-dating from time to time.

In evening devotions not so much time is spent on Bible study, but it is a time used for reviewing the day's activities, people met with, and prayers for members of the church and congregation. By using a visiting book or list of church members, taking a few families each day, one can be sure of remembering each individual or family. So often we write or say, 'I will remember you in prayer', but fail to do so. A system of regular prayer such as this one, ensures the intention becomes a real fact.

Our spiritual lives are also fed by reading good books. Biographies and devotional books help us overcome staleness and revitalise our spirits. They remind us that others have trekked this pilgrim path before us and their experience can help us on our own journey.

As my wife and I have grown together in the Lord's service, we have been greatly helped through Retreats and other such devotional programmes. Through the speakers at these events, or even through colleagues also attending, challenges have come to us leading to self examination, apologies for faults and a renewed determination to persevere, especially in areas of difficult relationships. We do not claim perfection, that is no doubt a long way off for us all, but we are led to increasing joy in service and satisfaction in our partnership.

Jesus said to those closest to Him, "Watch and pray that you may not enter into temptation; the spirit indeed is willing, but the flesh is weak." (Matt.26:41). He knew that none of His followers would be exempt from temptation. As His habit was daily prayer, it is clear we need to follow His example and take His advice.

Preparing for Worship

The notice over the counter of the bank read "Work is Worship". It was intended as an incentive to careful and efficient work. It can also be applied to our subject, for if worship is to be meaningful, a lot of work needs to be put into preparation. When does preparation begin? In a sense, it is going on all the time. Being aware of God everywhere and anytime is a preparation for worship, and can be an act of worship, too. As we speak with people, read a good book or even watch T.V., we can be gathering material that can contribute to worship on Sunday, though it has to be sorted out and thoughtfully used.

Corporate worship is a variable activity. Children can worship, and so can the elderly, but they will be best helped by different styles. Those facing danger need to worship as also do those whose lives seem to be untroubled. Sensing God's presence and responding to Him in reverence, repentance and obedience is essential to worship. Forms of worship can vary, sometimes meditative, sometimes very lively. In some churches there is a firmly set form service, often with the help of printed booklets. These set forms help the worshippers and leaders to know where they are going and permit prayers to be prayed aloud together. The danger is in so using the set form that it becomes monotonous and lifeless. Other churches avoid set forms to the point of carelessness; that, too, does not assist the worshippers. Before serving in a united church, I had never regularly used a lectionary and, indeed, was somewhat suspicious of the idea of a set theme for every Sunday. Later, I came to appreciate its help in keeping before me the vista of the Christian Year, Advent and Christ's coming, His life and ministry, the Cross and Easter, the gift of the Spirit and the continuing work of the Church. But let the lectionary be as intended, – a guide and a pointer. It should never become a chain.

Sometimes services have to be quickly devised, but the best services are usually those which are well prepared, and preparation should begin weeks ahead, – two weeks is the minimum. I remember enjoying a delightful meal of freshly cooked uppma with all the trimmings and being told that the mixture had to be prepared the previous day and allowed to ferment. It is something like this with a service and with a sermon. The sermon will be dealt with in the next chapter, but for both service and sermon it will be helpful if, having chosen the theme and tentatively selected some of the material, this can be set aside to ferment! We are told that our sub-conscious minds continue to work even when we are asleep. As we need to give time to prepare a sermon, in the same way a fair proportion of time needs to be given to preparing the whole service. From the moment a minister walks into the church until the final 'amen' at the end, the minister should be prepared for every aspect of the worship service.

Normally, there is an ebb and flow in worship which can be described as 'Approach to God' and 'Response to God'. Within the approach would come:

(i)   Gathering together the thoughts of all present and, usually through a verse of scripture, reminding the congregation of the presence of God whom they are seeking to worship. This leads to –

(ii) Praise to God for what He is and what He has shown Himself to be. Thanks may also be given to Him.

(iii) Awareness of His presence usually makes worshippers aware of personal unworthiness, failures and sin, so these need to be confessed with repentance. The basis of the New Covenant in Jesus Christ and the assurance of forgiveness are recalled.

Some may say that 'Response to God' has already started in (iii) above, which is true in a way. But in order to develop the flow of Response, we can –

(iv) Listen to God through scripture and think about its meaning and application to our lives; then

(v) Personal dedication and thanks may follow along with bringing gifts. Regular proportionate giving is part of our response.

(vi) An awareness of the needs of others and prayers for them fits in here. Even the Notices, or some of them (a subject dealt with in Chapter 10) may be involved with Response.

(vi) Finally there is a conclusion to corporate worship and a 'going out' – not going out of God's presence, for thankfully God is to be known outside our church buildings – but we do go out strengthened by Him to serve Him, and the Benediction will remind us of the fact.

Scripture, song and silence are all part of this ebb and flow of worship. Scripture is not only to be read for instruction and exposition, but can be used for praise and thanksgiving, and to express our confession, repentance and assurance of forgiveness. In choosing hymns, it is usual to have in mind the flow and the theme of the service, but let me share a piece of advice given to me by a friend. He said, "Don't choose all your hymns to fit in with your theme. Remember, when you are feeling joyful, others may be sad; when you are full of confidence, some, may be in great doubt or uncertainty! So include various aspects in your choice of hymns." Because the end of worship is as important as the beginning, we note that a well-sung hymn may nicely 'wrap up the package'. It can also be dangerous, if it gives people the feeling that they have now taken sufficient action. Nothing could be further from the truth. The congregation and minister should leave the church aware that they are just beginning their response.

Silence is not often used in public worship. Perhaps more use of it would allow us to examine our lives, actions and motives, and to give thanks, and think about words of scripture. It has been said that we are too 'wordy' in our worship. We seem to fear silence and want to fill all the gaps with words. It is good to wait on God in silence, so that we can hear what He is saying through our minds to our consciences and our senses. Yet, to help people use a time of silence effectively, a list of topics can be quietly suggested to them.

Prayer is a time for talking to God and listening to Him. It is not an opportunity to get across a point to the congregation. The sermon is the place for preaching! I have found it useful to note the different aspects of prayer and to keep these, to some extent, separate from each other. There is:

Praise - when we tell God of His greatness and graciousness; or 'Tell God how good He is and how much we love Him.'

Thanks often gets mixed up with praise, which is understandable, for we can thank God for all that we know of Him, for His gift in Christ and for all other things He has given.

Repentance and Confession often go together, and may be in words of scripture or hymns.

Intercessions - are when we bring the needs of others before God, never forgetting that He knows such needs better than we do;

Petition - when we speak to God of our own needs.

Dedication - personal commitment of others or oneself to God. So there are different aspects of prayer, and the minister has to be ready to guide the prayers of the congregation. Our prayers can be too general. For instance, instead of praying generally week by week for 'Justice and Peace' or for 'all labourers and craftsmen', would it not be as well to mention known areas of conflict or specific persons?

When preparing for worship, we need to remember that the concentration span of people is shorter than most ministers suppose. Many minsters do not realise that quite a few in the congregation have 'switched off' by the time the sermon comes. Which is to be preferred, ten minutes with the sense of the presence and purpose of God, or a hundred minutes of verbal activity? There are several ways of keeping the service alive and helping people to concentrate. One is to keep worship in small sections, another is to invite people's participation by asking them to join in a response following each prayer, or by having a change of voice to read passages of scripture. The same voice throughout a service can tend to monotony.

Another help to concentration is by telling people the structure of the service so that they can understand where they are going. Even where there is a set order of service in a prayer book, I have found it helps to supplement this with a cyclostyled Order of Service which will show the passages of scripture to be read, the hymn numbers, a synopsis of the sermon, or at least its topic, heading and text. Such a leaflet can include a prayer for the worshipper to use as preparation for worship and another prayer for use in the week ahead. The week's notices can also be printed along with concerns such as names of people for whom prayer is requested, jobs to be done, brief reports on the success (or otherwise) of projects, suggestions for good books to be read. In taking such a leaflet away with them, each member of the congregation will have opportunity for further reflection on the sermon and reminders of some of the responses that can be made.

Much of what I have said may appear to have relevance only for town congregations with little application to village situations. Village life seems to be much more casual and less organised. Children, and sometimes adults, drift in and out of the church during worship, and there is, always a background of village noise. Because of a seeming casualness, the minister should in no way be careless about conduct of worship. In village worship, we must give the best we can. This means understanding the villager's situation and preparing our material so that it is relevant. Quite a few of our church and national leaders have begun life in village settings. A village congregation is worthy of a well prepared and well conducted service.

To sum up – note down material for worship as it comes to you in daily life. Allow adequate time for preparation, which need not be done all at one time. Choose scripture readings and hymns with care. Be aware of time and avoid rambling. Most important of all, do all with prayer; prayer before, prayer during and prayer after preparation.

Preparing a Sermon

In this chapter we will consider how to prepare a sermon, including Introduction and Conclusion. Other aspects such as Selecting a topic, Illustrations, Filing sermons, Avoiding repetition, follow in the next chapter.

One of the most daunting experiences I can remember from seminary days was Sermon Class. On Friday mornings the entire college, staff and students, assembled and one of the students would have to preach a sermon on a text of his own choosing. That was bad enough, but afterwards the preacher had to sit with his fellow students and listen to a critical appraisal of the sermon, its content, manner of delivery, doctrinal accuracy, his appearance, mannerisms, strengths and weaknesses. I dreaded the day when my turn would come. On one occasion, vacation dates intervened and I was saved from the ordeal, but eventually and inevitably it came. There was no avoiding it. As it happened, the following week there was to be a general election, and to me this suggested a topical start. I chose the text from I Peter 1:10: "Therefore, brethren, be the more zealous to confirm your call and election. . .", contrasting the two types of election and encouraging my hearers to obedience and good works. Much time was spent preparing that sermon. It was rehearsed at length and, on the appointed day was preached to the assembly. That was the easy bit. The time that followed was harrowing. My theme was carefully examined , my scheme of presentation was pulled into shreds and the whole effort was declared a shambles. As far as I can remember, the only good thing said was that probably I was sincere in my intention! Later that day, at a soccer match, the assistant principal passed by and still warm from his morning's work, kindly asked me how I felt. My reply was something along the line of "Shattered!". "Well, never mind" was his encouragement, "You need to think the whole thing through carefully again. We've all made mistakes, you know!" So, knowing I was not to be entirely cast into outer darkness, I was left to lick my wounds.

It was a shattering experience, but I needed it, and we will need such things to help us realise that in preaching we tread on holy ground and that we go into the pulpit not to preach 'ourselves' or our own ideas, but to make the gospel plain.

Broadly speaking, there are two aims for preaching. Either it is to help Christian people deepen their faith, or it is to help non-Christian people understand the gospel. In both cases the type of audience or congregation will determine the way in which the sermon is presented. Children would need one style, elderly folk another, forces personnel yet another.

Having said that, the procedure for preparation is similar in any case. Your aim is to take a verse or a passage from the Bible and open it up for your hearers. Difficult words and concepts need to be explained, e.g. Sadducees, or Justification, and as we cannot explain words or meanings until we ourselves have understood them, we need to be disciplined students. We have to do two things, – study the Bible and also learn the truth through experience. In preaching we are sharing an experience, not presenting a theory. Thoughtful preparation will save us from random statements and rambling sermons. On very rare occasions we may have to speak on the spur of the moment, but always we shall be better understood if we are well prepared.

Because of the limitations of our own preaching ability, the concentration span of the average listener (10 -15 minutes) and the limited time of a normal church service, concentrate on ONE MAIN TOPIC per sermon. If a passage of scripture tends to lead from one topic to another, let the various subjects develop into a series of sermons. It is better to make one point adequately, than have five points that are lost to the listeners!

Preaching a sermon is like taking a boat load of people across a river. First you have to make sure they are with you and that you are heading in the right direction. Then you make steadily for the landing stage on the other side, and at the conclusion of the journey you can all look back and see from where you have come. Then you can expect the people to disembark feeling that they have been helped on their journey.

You will find it helpful to keep one notebook or have one file in which you jot down verses, themes or topics that appeal to you. Sometimes these will 'pop out' at you during personal devotions. Sometimes the subject will be presented to you by the lectionary reading for the day. Note such verses and subjects in your book or file, along with the thoughts that immediately occur to you. Then leave them. You will find that, because of your interest in the passage, your mind will be working on it while you are doing something else. The next time you pick up your notebook and turn to the page, several new angles and ideas will suggest themselves. Sometimes the verses which seemed so interesting one day will later appear as 'dead things'. In which case don't worry, but just leave them.

When the time comes for serious preparation, which may take

two or three sessions, look over all your notes and work out the main thrust of the sermon. Keep that goal always in front of you. Just as the wind or the river's current may carry a boat off course, so unnecessary deviations will not help you or your hearers. You may have to come back to a sermon several times and do a lot of revision and editing. Be ruthless in cutting out material which, although it may be interesting, deflects thought away from the main aim. Also use simple words when preaching. Jesus, in His preaching and parables used simple words that everyone could understand. We should follow His example.

For the benefit of their listeners, many preachers divide their sermons into three points. This is because most people can retain three well-made points, but find it difficult to recall seven! Sometimes, two points will be sufficient, and sometimes four. It will depend upon the text and upon the preacher, but three is a number easily handled. Somewhere in the sermon the truth found in the Bible will have to be applied to everyday situations. Such application may be made during each point of the sermon, or sometimes it will come mainly at the end. In any case the listeners must be helped to apply the truth of scripture to their own lives. So, write down possible sub-headings for each point of the sermon and assemble your ideas under the appropriate heading.

Phrase your sermon so that you do not preach at people. Let it be 'us' and 'we' rather than 'I' and 'you', otherwise listeners will get the impression the preacher is putting himself on a pedestal and will tend to reject the message.

Now a word about starting and finishing. The Introduction must be that and no more. It must serve the purpose of bringing your listeners attention to the subject of the sermon. Avoid long stories, funny jokes and excuses for not being ready! Make it simple. If possible, make it topical. You may find that something from a newspaper or a recent radio broadcast will help focus people's attention on the subject. You are not obliged to always give your text first, but it may be a great help.

At the conclusion of the sermon, do not keep circling round, finding more little bits to add on. Bring the boat nicely into the landing stage, allow the people to look back along the route they have taken and appreciate the point they have reached, then shut off the engine and allow them to continue their journey.

Here are examples of texts and what they suggest to me by way of sermon outlines. You may well look at these texts in a different way. Preachers are individuals and they do not all use one pattern. However, because it may help some, these examples are given:

(1) The very first words of the Bible: "In the beginning, God. . ." Genesis 1:1 makes a basic affirmation. Why was this necessary? Perhaps because while Hebrew people could look back on a God who had brought them out of nothing to make them into a special people for His purpose, there were many other religious people who saw the beginning of things as a duel between a god of light and a god of darkness, or between a warrior and a dragon. So our God is introduced as:

Personal - He is not mere 'Force' but the divine Super Person.

Progressive - note the different stages of creation, each one good, until man is brought on the scene and put in charge.

Purposeful - History not only has a beginning, it moves on to an end, where fellowship with God and morals matter. Even the possibility of sin thwarting His purpose does not stop God. A key role in God's opposition to sin is seen in the ministry of Jesus Christ. Here is a door through which we pass by faith into a new life.

Conclusion: Every Christian person can look back on a time when God intervened in his or her life. Each one can say, "I am what I am because God took the initiative." (which is another way of saying 'In the beginning, God. . .'). What has a beginning also has an end. The Bible also teaches us: 'In the end, God.' If we let God begin and continue His work in us, we shall be with God at the end, also. Quote Philippians 1: 6, and finish.

   (2) The Lord's Prayer. (Matt.6:7-15; or Luke 11:2-4). This could be the subject of two or more sermons;

The first dealing with verses 9 & 10 (or v.2 in Luke).

God's Holiness He is awesome. He is to be revered. (Exodus 3:5) (Exodus 19:22). Do we approach Him too casually?

God's Relationship To Christ He was 'Papa'. We, too, can call Him 'Father' (see John 20:17).

God's Kingdom What is His Kingdom? The Kingdom comes afresh to each generation. Are we ready to work as well as to pray for this to happen?

The second sermon would relate to verses 11-15 (Lk. 11:4):

(1) Daily basic needs

Such as bread, which God knows we need. Note how Jesus had compassion on people and fed them. What do we do to feed others in Christ's name?

(2) The matter of Forgiveness

There is a need to forgive others that we can ourselves know forgiveness. What is the result of not forgiving? Is it important for everyone? Is there someone I should forgive?

(3) The matter of Temptation

Temptation itself is not sin. Note how Christ was tempted.

What result did this have for Him? (Hebrews 4:15). Temptation, if resisted, can actually strengthen a person.

Why should one pray to be delivered from it? Because it provides a door through which we can step out from the gracious presence of God, offend God and thwart His purposes and separate ourselves from Him.

Each of these three sections deals with an important aspect of a Christian's life, and could become three sermons, e.g.:

(A) "DAILY NEEDS" - Bread is basic; luxuries not mentioned.

   - 'Give us' must go alongside 'We're willing to work'.

   - We must be ready to provide 'basics' for others.

(B) "FORGIVENESS" - Why is forgiveness necessary?

   - Why is forgiveness difficult?

   - How is forgiveness obtained?

(C) "TEMPTATION" - It is common to all.

   - It is dangerous.

   - It can bring a blessing!

Sermons (Part II) - Bits and Pieces

IS IT TO BE A SERMON, A HOMILY, OR AN ADDRESS?

In some churches, the minister tends to deliver a homily rather than a sermon. What is the difference between the two? In some cases there may be very little difference. A homily is often interesting, it is meant to be helpful, but it may not be based on scripture at all. A homily may deal with such matters as 'How to face illness when it comes?' 'Is it right to help older people?' or, 'The need for a new church hall.' There is nothing wrong with a homily, but as the hearing and understanding of the word of God is an essential part of normal worship, the exposition of scripture is the function of a sermon. A homily is usually quite short, perhaps five to ten minutes, and therefore it may be more popular with a congregation than a sermon! If a homily seeks to make the meaning of scripture clear, e.g. ' The attitude of Jesus towards poverty.' or 'Who are the poor in spirit?', then it has a place in worship. If, however, the purpose of a homily is to call for volunteers to help with the church fete, it had better be treated as part of the Notices and should not take the place of a sermon. Sermons are meant to be preached and to present the meaning of scripture in such a way that the listeners are stirred to action. Some may avoid preaching a sermon because not only does it take a lot of preparation, but it may give the impression of knowing all the answers or convey a sense of superiority. It is right to avoid a know-all attitude, but as preacher and congregation explore scripture together it can be a sharing in fellowship.

An address can be very like a homily, but need have no religious content at all. I would think of an address as dealing, for example, with 'Experiences of travel in Central Africa' or 'What is right with caste' or 'How to care for fearful children.'

CHOOSING A TEXT FOR A SERMON

This can be one verse, a chapter, or it can be a subject that is dealt with in several places in the Bible, such as 'Lamb of God' or 'The peace of God'. In the latter case, do not quote all the passages but be selective. Sometimes try a series of sermons, for example on the Beatitudes (Matthew 5:3-10) or The Lord's Prayer (Matt.6:7-15). Each can provide material for an interesting series of five or six sermons. If you decide to attempt a series, then consider whether to present the series week by week or whether to split up the series into say two Sundays per month. It depends on whether the congregation's interest can be sustained. Too much of a good thing may give your hearers indigestion! In any case, before you choose a text and before you get to work on the text, take time for prayer because we need to ask God to guide our minds and choices at each stage.

MY FAVOURITE THEME

Some preachers have a fondness for certain texts or subjects. Things like Repentance or Commitment or Helping the poor may come again and again. Examine your own record to see whether you tend to repeat some themes and neglect others. It will help, if you keep a record of your own sermons and then look back over a year and search for many omissions. You may often speak about the Love of God, but have you presented the Judgement of God also? We like to speak of New Life in

Christ, but do we ever deal with a Christian view of death? One advantage of being guided by a lectionary is that throughout each year a wide range of subjects is presented by the selected scripture passages.

SHOULD SERMONS BE KEPT OR RE-USED?

There is no reason why a sermon should not be preached more than once, but it has to be presented in a fresh way. So the 'old' material has to be carefully reviewed and the 'fire stirred up'. But try not to repeat the same sermon to the same congregation, – they just might remember!

WHAT TO DO WITH OLD SERMONS?

Some may seem dry enough to burn well! But from what has been said above, it is plain that it is useful to file old sermons. There are many ways of doing this, but let me describe two methods. One is to keep each manuscript in a separate envelope. On the outside of the cover write the sermon's title, the scripture reading on which it is based, and where and on what date it was preached. If re-used, the further details can be noted on the same envelope. Another method is to file the manuscript in a loose-leaf file and write on the back of the paper the details of date and place.

ILLUSTRATIONS AND STORIES

Ministers often keep a collection of illustrations. These can be incidents observed during your daily life or can come from magazines, books and newspapers. It is wise to avoid using stories that identify local personalities. A card index may be used for filing illustrations. On the front of the card write the saying or story. On the back record the date, place and sermon title when used. This means discipline in record keeping but it will be very useful. It will provide a store of material to which you can turn, and it will help you not to repeat the same story in the same place. The cards can be sorted and filed in groups, each group relating to a different subject such as Adversity,

Bible, Cheating, Jesus, Justice, Prayer, Salvation, Stewardship etc.

SPECIAL OCCASIONS

Occasions such as dedications, baptisms, marriages and funerals provide special opportunities. Among the visitors to such services may be non-Christians as well as Christian friends. There is the opportunity to present basic Christian truths. For instance, the message during a marriage service can point out what fidelity in marriage means, or how thoughtful caring for a partner is a Christian duty. An infant baptism or dedication provides an occasion for speaking of the needs and responsibilities that come with parenthood. At a memorial service it may be right to refer to the purpose of life, the best ways to use wealth and influence, to the need to live in a godly fashion, making sacrifices where necessary, so that life's achievements have eternal values, and the certainty that Christ gives us in the face of death. Because funerals and memorial services usually happen without warning, keep ready one or two short messages specially for such occasions. It is also necessary to be prepared for a funeral where the dead person has not been closely connected with the church. The person may be classed as a Christian for census purposes, but there may not have been evidence of Christian commitment during life. We are not called upon to judge, but we need to avoid false and flowery compliments.

AFTER PREACHING HAS FINISHED

At the end of a service it is usual for a pastor to greet people personally as they leave the church. At such times people may say "That was a lovely sermon pastor" or "Thank you so much for the message." Be careful not to accept flattery. People may not say all that they feel, and anyway, if there has been meaning in the message, this has been the work of the Holy Spirit. So how do you respond? You can say: "Thankyou for listening." or "Let's hold on this truth through the week." or

"Let us trust God to help us." It is worth remembering Proverbs 27:21, "The crucible for silver and furnace for gold. But man is tested by the praise he receives."

Many preachers feel disappointed at the end of a Sunday. They realise they have missed opportunities or have badly stated the truth, and they feel they are failures. While we admit most sermons could be better prepared and presented, and we have to note our errors and do better next time, we can also count on God to work in His way. He has an ability to take even our failures and use them to fulfill His purposes. So we keep to the word of God and rely upon the Holy Spirit to produce the harvest. When we feel our uselessness as Christ's servants, we can reflect on God's word in Isaiah 55:11 "So shall my word be. . .", or note the aftermath of failure in John 21:15-19, where the dejected Peter is not rejected, but told to: "Feed my lambs, tend my sheep. . ."

MANNERISMS WHILE PREACHING

Your best friends will be able to tell you the things that disturb them in the way you preach. It may be in matters of dress, where hair is uncombed, or gown or stole are awry, or clothes are creased; it may be in deportment, – the way you move around while talking, or you may appear to wash your hands while speaking; or it may be repetition of a phrase such as ". . . and so we see. . ." or "fundamentally. . ." or "Now let us think. . .". Such habits creep into our pulpit manner or vocabulary unnoticed by us, but wife or friends can perform a valuable service by noting such things and passing them on at a suitable time. Then it is up to the pastor not to justify himself but to note and correct the defect.

8

Pastoral Visiting

IS VISITING NECESSARY?

The pastor is a shepherd who needs to know his flock, and his people need to know more of God through him. A brief handshake at the door of the church on a Sunday morning, with all the congregation pressing around, does not provide the opportunity for sharing news or problems. The pastor who is seen only on Sundays and is invisible for the remaining six days in the week, quickly loses touch with the needs of his people and gains the reputation for not caring. His care for his people will be shown both through leading of worship and preaching of God's Word Sunday by Sunday, and by regularly visiting them at other times.

THE PURPOSE OF VISITING

As well as worshipping God, the Church is also concerned with fellowship. The pastor's visits (as well as those of Pastoral Visitors in churches which have them) extend the fellowship of the Church into the homes of Christ's people. Only by visiting can a pastor come to know the actual circumstances in which his people live, their problems, joys and talents. Visiting provides the opportunity to review blessings, receive suggestions and, when appropriate, give guidance. Because many people's sense of hospitality means they will want to provide some refreshment, to accept this may help to put them at their ease and can be an aid to conversation. However, food and drink is not essential to a visit, nor must such hospitality become a burden on the home.

The pastor does not visit in order to collect money, so avoid appearing to expect payment for your visit. However, some who are not able to get to church due to ill-health or some such reason, may wish to take the opportunity to send their contribution to church funds through the pastor. It is wise for the pastor to have a few blank envelopes, perhaps in his visiting book, into which such offerings can be placed and the name of the donor written in the outside. This will help him to remember where the money came from and avoid possible confusion with his own private finances.

Whenever possible, let every visit include a short time for scripture reading and prayer, with, if you are able, the whole family. Always prepare a few verses of scripture before setting out on your visit, so that your reading will have relevance for the people being visited.

A SYSTEM FOR VISITING

Unless the pastor has a definite system for visiting, it is all too easy to gravitate toward the homes where he feels most at ease and to avoid visiting 'difficult' parishioners – who, if visited more frequently, may become more supportive. There will, of course, always be those whose circumstances mean that they have priority for our visiting time. Those who are house-bound because of ill-health or have responsibility for caring for a sick or invalid person, need special attention. Some who are going through a time of crisis or facing a particular dilemma, may require regular visits for counselling over a period of time. Sudden emergencies or critical illness may mean that the pastor has to spend extra time with certain families. New people coming to worship should be visited as soon as possible, to know that you are interested in them. Let your visiting include non-christian friends. This helps to build bridges between communities and prevents the christian community from appearing insular and not interested in their neighbours.

Allowing for special needs, I suggest a system for visiting as follows. In arranging the week's schedule, let two evenings, if possible the same two evenings each week, be set aside for general visiting. Another two periods could be set aside for 'priority visiting', remembering that often for those who are ill or in hospital or are housebound, daytime rather than evening visiting may be more suitable. Occasionally, a whole morning may have to be given to a particular visit, but normally, it is better to give the first hours of the day when one is fresh and most alert, to the study. Much can be accomplished in two hours study and preparation and then between mid-morning tea and lunch there will be time for a hospital or home visit. Keeping the housebound and sick in mind, I found it was often helpful to visit on a Saturday afternoon when I was able to take with me a copy of the Order of Service for the next day. This would include the numbers of the hymns to be sung, the readings, perhaps a brief outline of the sermon and notices about future church activities. In this way, the sick person would be able to share in what was going on and feel included in the fellowship of the gathered church. If the person has a radio or tape-recorder, it may be possible to leave a recording of last week's service. Suggestions about times and wave-lengths when Christian radio programmes may be heard can also be a help. Often when I have been visiting a sick person in hospital and have had prayer with them, a patient in a neighbouring bed has asked for prayer also. Never refuse such an invitation. When praying with a patient in hospital, include non-christian patients and staff in your prayers. Some may be listening who will appreciate the prayer which can be offered with confidence 'through Jesus Christ' or 'in the name of

Christ'. Use the opportunity not to 'preach' at the patient, but to show the love of Jesus in whose name you will pray.

Having decided on the two evenings for regular visiting, you then need to know by what system you will ensure each member of the church will receive equal attention. The system that I have found most helpful is to keep a Visiting Book. This may be an ordinary notebook, or better still, a loose-leaf notebook into which extra pages can be placed as necessary. The pages are divided up allowing several pages for different streets or block of flats. It will take some time writing such a book, but in my experience, will prove very worthwhile. Allow space beside each family to record the names of all the children as well as the parents and note dates of birth beside the names of the children. Children like to be addressed by their names, and a quick look into the visiting book before going into a home will serve to remind the pastor, not only of the names of the children, but whether anyone has had or will soon have a birthday. One other thing I have found useful is to write the names of church members in blue ink, but names of others yet to join the church or other friends in the neighbourhood in a different colour. So the pages of your visiting book may look like this:-

Page 1. BAZAR AREA

House	Names	Phone
21 Gautam Rd	Mr. & Mrs. S.P. Massey	711058
	d. Meena (b, 12.2.84)	
	s. Mohan (b, 6.12.86)	
27a	Mr. & Mrs. J.B. Singh.	
	s. Samuel (b, 10.5.75, bap,1.8.92)	

| 14 Market Pce | Mr. Sohan B. Lal | 711331 (9-5) |
| 12 Aliganj | Mr. John Dass | c/o 713003 |

Page 2. CIVIL LINES

| 2 Central Rd | Nurses Hostel | 712576 |

Rm.21 Miss Shanti Singh (Confirmed 5/4/92)

63 Miss Shobha Naidu

42 Miss Stella Solomon

13 Green Ave. (S/Qrs)

| (c/o S.K. Sharma) | Atul Kumar |

B. Bapu

| 87 (St. Marys Home) | Mrs. S. Dutta | (Office) | 715012 |
| | (Matron) | | |

d. Bina (b. 17.9.82)

Mrs. Molly J. Dass (Residents)715079

By following a system as outlined above, visiting area by area, you will be able to announce to the congregation the previous Sunday, which areas you intend to visit in the coming week. Do not allow callers to frustrate your planned visits. You can tell them that you have a prior engagement. Only real emergencies should hinder your visiting, and if you have to cancel visits, try to inform those who are expecting you. Tell them of your regret, and visit them as soon as possible.

WHEN NOT TO VISIT.

There are times when the pastor is not welcome. For example, if there are guests in the house or a special family celebration is taking place. Homework may be in progress or the family may be having their evening meal. Be sensitive to such matters. Go on to the next visit and offer to return later, or on another day. Such sensitivity to the situation is as indicative of your caring for the family as is the visit itself.

Again, when children are alone in the house, or a young daughter is there by herself, it is best to decline any polite invitation to come in. Rather, ask when the parents will be back and return on another day. When visiting single working women who appreciate and need a pastoral visit, or a married woman who is at home while her husband is away, try to take another suitable person with you, and so save your parishioner from the possible gossip of neighbours. (This is a situation where a visit from the pastor along with his wife may be the answer.)

LETTING PEOPLE KNOW

Some of the difficulties mentioned above may be avoided if people are aware in advance of your intention to visit. An advertised programme of visiting through the church bulletin board or in the church notices will allow those living in the area to be visited to let you know if it will be inconvenient. Three or at the most four homes are all that you will manage in one evening and your people will appreciate knowing that you are likely to visit them on a particular evening. It will also save you much wasted time and disappointment from knocking on doors and getting no answer. However, there will be times when you do call at a house and find no one in. Put a note through the door or leave a printed card to let it be known that you have called. It is worth the trouble and expense of having such cards printed. People do appreciate knowing that they have not been forgotten, even though they may not have been at home to receive you.

HAZARDS OF VISITING.

I know of one colleague who, if he found the television on in

the home he was visiting and the family made no move to turn
it off, took his chair and sat in front of the screen, so making
viewing impossible! This seems to me to be just as rude as the
act of leaving the set on, and hardly the way to start a pastoral
visit. However, it has to admitted that the television can cause
problems for the visitor. It may be that, if the programme has
only a short while to run, then one can sit with the family to
allow them to see the end of their programme. At other times,
a polite request that the set be turned off for a short time, is
accepted. But, if there is obvious reluctance to part with the
T.V. programme, then it is best not to stay, but to give a greeting
and pass on to another house – where they may be fortunate
enough not to own a T.V.!

Dogs! If you are frightened by dogs, they sense it and give you
a rough welcome. Most dogs mean no harm, but if one does
appear to be regarding you as an unwanted intruder, it is best
to stand still until one of the family rescues you. Never turn and
run, because the animal will then regard you as fair game and
may bite.

Children, these can hardly be described as hazards, but there
are certain things to be aware of when children are present.
It is always a delight to have the children there when visiting
a family but do realise that they are listening to all that is being
said and may well repeat garbled versions of a conversation
and so cause misunderstandings. Save confidential matters for
another occasion, or be very guarded in what you say.
Children can be very hurt by the way we speak about them in
their presence. On one occasion, when introducing me to the
family, the lady of the house, to my horror, said, " This is my
son. See how dark he is!". Such thoughtless remarks can be
very hurtful to the child and the pastor needs to make quick
and comforting response such as, "I think dark people are very
nice" or "Thank God that He loves us whatever our colour",
or quote from the Bible and say, "The Song of Solomon speaks

of dark person as being comely". This will take the sting out of the hurtful words and give the child a positive attitude to himself. Your kindness will be remembered as representing the attitude of the Saviour who loves each one.

VISITING PEOPLE WHO ARE ILL

"Father, am I going to die?" This was the question one young person put to me as she lay on her hospital bed. At the time, I hoped she would recover and I sought to reassure her, but as I read a few verses of scripture and prayed with her, I reminded her that Jesus has promised to be with His people always, and that day or night, whether we are conscious or asleep, we are always present with our Lord. Later I was thankful that I had been led to speak in this way, as the youngster died within a few hours of my visit. The tendency when visiting the sick is always to deny the possibility of death. Of course we need to stress the positive approach and pray for and look for recovery, and we would always try to encourage the patient in faith and hope. But to deny the possibility of death is to suggest that our faith cannot cope with the event. We value good health and together with medical personnel we work for recovery, but nevertheless our Saviour is a risen Saviour and thus the victor over death. Sometimes we have to be with people in their last hours in this world and the minister has to watch with them and pass them over to Christ who is both this side and that side of death.

In this connection, we note that people from different backgrounds have different attitudes to receiving Holy Communion when they are ill. Some regard it as equal to receiving the last rites and as a signal that they are not expected to live. Others find it an extension of the fellowship of the Lord's Table, feel included in the membership of the Church and are strengthened by the bread and wine and the invisible presence of Christ. This latter view is the view I have and I would encourage those who are ill to receive Holy Communion regularly, but we do need to be careful for those who would find it anything but a comfort.

It helps those who are ill to know that the gathered Church is praying for them, and if it is possible, to record the Sunday worship service and leave the recording for the sick person to listen to after your visit, then the sense of being part of the fellowship is enhanced. The content of a previous week's tape may become a centre for discussion or conversation on your next visit.

You will find it useful to have verses marked in your Bible that are of particular comfort to those who are ill. A useful selection of such verses is given in the CNI booklet 'The Ministry to the Sick'. Keep your own personal copy of this or another such booklet and mark in it the passages you find particularly useful. Other passages of your own choice can be added at the back of the booklet. Always pray with the patient, but remember to keep your prayer short as a sick person cannot usually sustain a long period of concentration. Do not stay too long. Usually a ten-minute visit is long enough and will not over-tire your parishioner. If an unknown patient requests prayer, always make time for this.

VISITING THE BEREAVED

Sometimes it is the pastor who has to break the news of the death of a loved one. Though this is never an easy thing to do, who better to do it than a 'brother in Christ'? We do not, of course, do this in our own strength or wisdom, but count on the Holy Spirit to guide our words. The pastor should never forget the gravity of the situation or the shock which death causes for relatives. At first it is difficult for people to grasp the fact that a loved one has gone. It takes time for the fact to sink into their minds. Then, weeping and crying out is to be expected. The presence of the pastor is usually a great comfort at such times, even though he may not say very much. Indeed, silence is better than careless words such as "It can't be helped", or "Don't worry, you will get over it" which can be like stab wounds to a person already grievously hurt. To sit silently with a person allowing them to talk, may be the best ministry for the moment.

Be caring in practical ways. At such times as bereavement, people lose their power to think straight. Some will want to fast until after the burial, but gentle persuasion to drink or eat just enough to avoid faintness may be necessary. Finding a member of the family or a close friend who will take the responsibility of contacting the undertaker and making the funeral arrangements may be necessary. The pastor is often the one who will know who to contact in these necessary practical arrangements and will be able to supply names and telephone numbers for the cemetery, etc. There may be messages to be sent to relatives and arrangements to be made for the immediate care of young children. The pastor is not expected to undertake these tasks himself, but can give guidance to the family when their state of shock prevents them thinking of such details. When leaving for the burial, a reminder to someone to close and lock the windows and doors of the house and so avoid giving an unscrupulous person the opportunity to take advantage of the grieving family, is just another small way in which the pastor, from his wider experience of bereavement, can minister to his people. At certain times, it may be that the pastor can shield the family against intrusion by the press or inquisitive neighbours, and it is always wise to be guarded over any comments made to reporters or to onlookers. It is after the funeral is over and the relatives have departed that the sense of loss and loneliness is at its most acute. The pastor and his wife or a rota of church members can help by keeping up regular contact with the family in the weeks following the funeral. Such ministry will help build up the church, as members are brought into closer, caring fellowship with each other.

The Church at Leisure

Church services are usually rather formal with rites and rituals. These can be most impressive, but if pastor and people only meet under such circumstances, they will never know each other personally. We all need to know each other as we really are and the pastor and his family need to be known as real people who can laugh and have fun, who can play games – and may be very good at them too. There must be times when the pastor and his people can meet together without formality and when ordinary every-day language is used.

"All work and no play makes Jack a dull boy" says a western proverb, and this can be true of the Church. If times of relaxed fellowship and enjoyment together are stimulating for the life of the congregation and brings greater understanding among the members and appreciation of each other, then it is essential that there should be such opportunities. These occasions do not just happen themselves. They have to be planned and included in the church's schedule.

The most obvious and easiest opportunity for fellowship is following worship, perhaps over a cup of tea. However, all too often this becomes a time when friends meet together in their own little groups and any strangers present are ignored. This may not be intentional, but care needs to be taken to see that all are included in the fellowship. This is a situation where a rota of members can be given the task of attending to hospitality. It is, of course, natural that friends will want to meet each other and share their news. Therefore, in order to open up the groups and lower the barriers of ethnic or language divisions, more extended times of fellowship must be organised.

Special occasions such as a church anniversary may be celebrated not only by special worship services, but also by having a congregational meal. For some, the whole enjoyment seems to focus on a big cooking job, and no one can question the pleasure of eating a satisfying meal together. But this means a lot of hard work for a few and involves expense that may cause problems for some families. If each family brings a picnic lunch, enough for themselves and one other person, there can be equal pleasure in sharing and appreciating the variety of food. Part of the role of the pastor on these occasions is to see that no one feels left out or ignored. Being aware of the lonely ones and the strangers, and introducing them to others in the fellowship is part of the purpose of the get-together. Also the person whose circumstances mean that his contribution to the 'feast' is only rice or makkhan-roti can be terribly hurt, if his package is left untouched and eventually thrown away. Jesus set us an example in His gathering up of the left-overs, and we do well to follow His lead.

One drawback to the after-church picnic is that one may not be wearing clothes that suit both worship and picnic. So, planning for a church outing or picnic on another day, perhaps a public holiday, is a good idea, though popular picnic spots are crowded on such days. It is not necessary to travel far to enjoy oneself. The church may be set in a large compound where it is easy to make all the arrangements. Or, for a change of scenery, a park within walking distance may be a convenient location. If you decide to travel to some beauty spot 20 or 30 miles away, then it is necessary to plan carefully for transport, food, drink and to budget carefully so that everyone will know the cost of the trip. Make it possible for even the poorest family to share fully in the day. A badly organised outing can turn what should be a delight into a disaster. Responsibilities need to be shared and this often reveals unsuspected talent among church members. The areas of responsibilities to be covered will include:

(i)   Getting people to and from the site;

(ii) Organising refreshments, including adequate drinking water;

(iii) Providing for music, singing;

(iv) Arranging games (separate group for young children) and competitions;

(v) Arranging a speaker, or leading a short epilogue;

(vi) Finance, Budget, and how to collect the money;

(vii)Overseeing the total programme; (This does not necessarily have to be done by the pastor).

(viii)First Aid Box.

A day of fun and games, however, is not the only way to relax and get to know each other. A church Retreat or Study Day where there is opportunity to discuss, to share and explore new ideas is a valuable way of bringing people closer together and increasing appreciation of each other. It is often surprising to find how wrong our judgement of others has been when our meetings have been confined to a passing 'namaste' on Sunday morning. Choose a topic that is relevant and of interest to the people, may be The Bible, Prayer, or Homelessness. Use a film or bring in a reliable speaker to introduce the subject. Don't let the day be too heavy, but allow for some relaxation. If you have two sessions sitting down and thinking, then you will need a session of movement and activity. This could be a workshop on the use of skits and drama in worship, or new games to use in youth work, and there will certainly be much fun and laughter among the participants in such sessions.

While it is true that learning is best done in relaxed surroundings, it is also true that people differ in their interests and capabilities. To study is excellent, but not everybody is used to mental exercise. Just to relax and enjoy each other's company is also a learning experience. We learn that religion is more than worship services and that talents have been distributed to many people, talents that are only discovered by providing the opportunities for people to use them. Above all, we learn that the Church is alive and active, not just for two hours on a Sunday, but for all the other 166 hours in a week.

A pastor in a village will tackle this need in a different way. His people may be working in the fields and even on a Sunday there may not be leisure time for games. A village congregation may well hesitate before putting any time or money into a mela. But there are annual feasts and traditions which permit a day of leisure here and there. The pastor will be wise to plan ahead and help make the day a special one for his people; games for the children, competitions for the youth, music and coloured paper flags, and special food. A teaching story with visual aids will live in peoples memories for a long time, and with a little forethought and help from others, a Life of Christ film could be shown. It may be only after a year that the success of the day becomes apparent, – when someone says 'Pastor, can we do that again?'

So far we have been thinking of the congregation spending leisure time together and the benefits that accrue. We need also to think about the pastor's leisure time, and that of his wife and family. Because it is necessary for the pastor to be 'on duty' at times when others may be enjoying some leisure, it is to be expected that the pastor's own leisure time will necessarily be when others are working. This is not always understood by the congregation. It is essential that the congregation should be informed and helped to appreciate and co-operate in this matter. For example, if it is known that the pastor's day off is Tuesday, then the congregation will, except in an emergency, see that he is not called upon for church affairs on that day. An uninformed congregation can be unjustly critical when they see their pastor off for a day's fishing just when they are having to fight their way on to a crowded bus. It is also true, however, that a congregation will tend to measure their pastor's need for relaxation against the quality of effort and the time he puts into his pastoral duties. It means that every pastor has to be careful how he spends his time when he is 'on duty'.

And what about his wife? There is a sense in which it is never possible for a housewife or mother, especially one who has a job apart from her church responsibilities, to be 'off duty', and so it is even more essential for her that she gets a break. An off-duty day is also important for the whole family. Children need to know that there is at least one day a week when Mummy and Daddy belong to them! Personally, I found it convenient not to have a regular weekly day off, but to take time when it was needed. My children were in boarding school, so it was more useful for me to take time off when they were home for holidays, and I am grateful for a congregation that was understanding about this.

How many pastors and their families are able to get away for an annual holiday? We all find it refreshing to enjoy new surroundings sometimes, where the telephone doesn't ring and where we can plan our day's activities assured that they will not be interrupted. But getting away can be expensive, so, perhaps a church can be encouraged to make a contribution to holiday expenses for the pastor and his wife. It goes without saying, that the pastor, for his part, must merit this sort of consideration. If the pastor seems to enjoy leisure on most days of the week, then no one is likely to help with holiday costs.

An annual holiday needs planning, not only where to go and when, but for the pastor's responsibilities to be covered in his absence. Some duties may be taken on by members of the pastorate committee, but it will be necessary to arrange for a fellow minister to be available for such things as funerals, visiting the dying or other emergencies. By putting such arrangements in place before he leaves, the pastor shows his consideration for the church, and this will be appreciated.

Children and Young People

Two of our grandchildren were playing together in the garden when suddenly there came the sound of crying. Mark came running to his mother for solace, complaining "Tim hit me with a stone." After giving a comforting kiss to the hurting spot, the three-year old aggressor was called to account. Feeling the apparent injustice of being so strongly reprimanded, Tim said defensively "But that's what David did!". It became clear that the two boys had been playing at David and Goliath, one of their favourite Bible stories, and it was Goliath who had come in crying! Which just goes to show how Religious Education can affect a child at a very young age!

When does caring for the young in the church begin? I would encourage parents to bring their babies to church with them from the very begining. When a baby is brought to church, the people, the surroundings, the music, etc., all become part of the child's life and experience in the same way as home and family, friends and neighbours. Waiting until a child is 'old enough to behave' means introducing him or her to a strange new atmosphere at an age when there will be some difficulty in adjusting. Of course, this means that the church must recognise the special needs of parents with young children and make provision for them.

A crying child can be acutely embarrassing to the parents. Father may scowl at his wife implying that the disturbance is her fault. The mother may try all the child's best loved positions, only to meet with an increasing crescendo of yells. Mother and child need a way of escape, and this may be provided by a creche. If it is possible to find volunteers who will take turns in looking after the babies during service time this will be welcomed by parents who are then able to give their attention to worship. If a creche is not possible, then a room set aside where mothers can feed babies, and change nappies is helpful. It is often difficult for a mother to sit through a full hour of worship with a young child, but to be able to share in perhaps half the service, then sit in a comfortable room to wait for the rest of the family is a great help, and the child will gradually become accustomed to staying for longer periods of time in the church.

The service of Infant Baptism or Infant Dedication is a congregational event. (Is it the child who is dedicated, or is it the parents who dedicate themselves to the Christian upbringing of the child? - or both?). Gone, we hope, are the days of secluded gatherings when the child is brought to a seemingly secret ceremony. Rather, this is an occasion when parents can be seen and supported and know that they are linked up with a group of Christians who will continue to have the welfare of them and their child at heart. This is also an occasion when it is good to have the Sunday School children present. They will see and hear what takes place, will understand that each child matters, will hear the promises that Christian parents make concerning their children, and can be encouraged to share in the responsibilities of making all children feel at home in their church. For the pastor, along with the ceremony comes the need for careful paper-work. A definite and correct entry into the Register kept as a Church record, and a certificate for the parents to take home and keep in their family file, is a job that should not be put off until some time later. It is possible for the memory to play tricks and for errors to creep into the record. If the church really cares, then this register will provide a list of birthdays throughout the year when greetings can be given to the parents and children.

Early in my ministry, I started an anniversary register with a page for every day of the year. Each page had four sections. The first contained the names of children born on that day (with the year of their birth also written). The second section had the names of those confirmed or baptised as believers. In the third section were listed the marriages that had taken place on that day, and the final section had the names of those who had died. This proved useful for remembering birthdays and anniversaries, but it did take time to keep up to date and in the end I ceased keeping this record. I wish I had kept it going.

Sunday School is a vital part of the life of the church. It is not somewhere to send the children so that they do not disturb adults. It is the place where, together with a Christian home, the foundations of Christian discipleship are laid. A church should appreciate the need to provide the best possible resources for the Sunday School, remembering that the children are part of the church family and the church needs to see them and get to know them. To have the children present in the regular worship services for about ten minutes with a short address given especially for them, enables them to feel that they belong. Because a child's concentration span is short, do not expect them to sit quietly through a long introductory prayer. Save the long prayers until after the children have left for Sunday School.

Teachers, like all Christians, need spiritual nourishment, so if possible, aim at having two teachers per class so that they can alternate and each have opportunity to attend worship turn by turn. They also need lesson books to guide them and ensure that their teaching covers the various aspects of scripture and faith.

A pastor encourages his Sunday School teachers by recognising their worth and the value of the work that they do and by co-operating with them. Occasionally, by arranging for someone else to take over the service for a time, he can spend ten minutes on a Sunday morning with the children in Sunday School, showing his interest in what is being taught and seeing for himself some of the problems such as limited space or too few teachers for too many children, that his teachers face week by week. Regular meetings with the Sunday School teachers, say once every three months, enables him to hear their comments, share their joys and difficulties and plan programmes and outings. The pastor who does not show his interest in the Sunday School is, in effect, discouraging the teachers and missing the opportunity of contact with the children in their early years.

If Sunday School children take up an offering, they should know what happens to their money. Knowing that their money offered to God, will be used for such causes as helping children with leprosy or blind people, will encourage them in their giving and introduce them to the way God uses people and their resources. It will not be helpful to them to learn that their offerings are being spent on Teachers' Manuals or are being saved for their Christmas Party! This only teaches them to look after themselves and not to think of others.

Sunday School teachers appreciate training. This gives them confidence and ideas, and helps them to realise that the problems they have are common to all Sunday School teachers. The ISSU and the Christian Education department of EFI are willing to run courses for training Sunday School teachers and often several churches can get together to organise a course. Such an arrangement needs to be planned well ahead, as six months' or one year's notice may be necessary. Teachers will appreciate refresher courses and as new teachers will be coming into the Sunday School, such a course every three or four years is advisable. A church that is willing to provide finance enabling its teachers to share in training and refresher courses is showing appreciation of all that the teachers do and is also expressing its concern for the spiritual welfare of the children in its care. It is often the pastor who has the job of encouraging his members to provide this support to the Sunday School teachers.

For churches that have children available on a Sunday afternoon, a very useful idea is that of Bible Club for the 9-14 year olds. Such a programme can last for one hour or just over, with the time divided into four quarters. A different activity is arranged for each quarter, e.g.

1. A game involving physical movement.

2. A quiet game like Bible Acrostics or miming Bible characters.

3. Singing choruses or drawing.

4. Hearing a Bible story or seeing a Bible Film Strip.

Somewhere in the programme allow for simple light refreshments.

A register can be kept, and points awarded to the youngsters attendance, bringing a Bible, memory work and competitions. You will find such a programme becomes very popular with your children and before long they will want to bring their friends. If Bible Club can be held in a home, either the pastor's home or that of a church member, this will add to the programme's appeal.

Following Bible Club, young people can join Junior Youth Fellowship for the 15s - 17s. The Y. F. should be encouraged to take an active part in planning their own programme with a healthy balance between games and service projects. Within a framework of a four-week cycle, there can be

1) Going out visiting Homes for the Aged, Cottage meetings;

2) Games, varied according to needs;

3) Bible Study;

4) Talks by senior friends on serious topics. The young people themselves can suggest topics, speakers.

The important factor is adequate responsible leadership. If there is a reliable leader, the pastor need not always attend the sessions, but he should be present at planning and Youth Committee meetings. It is a good thing to allow the Manse to be used for such Committees, as it helps the young people feel at home with pastor and his wife.

Notices

There are still towns in India where public announcement is made by the dholak and town crier. The khatak-khatak of the drum causes people to listen because they know an announcement is to follow which might affect their livelihood. What a contrast to the public-address systems used at some railway stations. Either a series of clicks is followed by a voice so soft that it cannot be heard, or there is a bellowing sound that echoes around and around and so drowns in its own noise. Which all adds up to the fact that while announcements are necessary – sometimes vitally necessary – if people cannot hear and understand them, they are useless.

This applies to Church Notices. Many of them are necessary, some are routine, but unless they are understood they might just as well not be attempted. Also, it is necessary to ask which notices are necessary for worshippers.

The days and time of regular meetings? Do we need to be told that "next Sunday our worship will be at 10 a.m. and 6 p.m."? Most people can get by without such an announcement because either they already know the regular timings, or they can read them on the church Notice Board. But, if it is a case that "next Sunday our worship will begin an hour earlier", then everybody needs to be told. That a member has had to go into hospital or there has been a bereavement are matters that affect the fellowship, but could be most suitably announced prior to a time of prayer. Marriage Banns and Notice of the church's Annual General Meetings have, by rule, to be announced in public worship services. Church members need to know which area the pastor will be visiting in the coming week, but they can survive without being told how many points were scored by a church football team. Whether such matters are of interest to the members is one thing. That they assist them in devotions is another. Whatever is done 'in church' is usually part of a service of worship. We need to ask whether in a service of worship we are serving God or ourselves. If worship is directed towards God and His continuing work in creation, this will help determine which notices are included and which are not.

Many churches have a Notice Board which is a recognised and useful place to exhibit information such as, Times of Meetings, Visiting Speakers, Forthcoming Marriages, Invitations from other churches. Some churches produce a weekly news-sheet which each worshipper receives. By conveying information in this way, the pastor or secretary needs only draw attention to any special announcement.

Preparing a news-sheet solves a number of problems, except that of who is responsible for producing it! Very few churches have a typist, so it is quite usual for the pastor to be the one to write and arrange the duplication of the church news-sheet, which can include the order of service for the day. While this does add to his work load, it also provides the pastor with opportunity to vet announcements ahead of time. It allows him to set a dead-line for receiving notices. This he can quote when someone rushes up to him just as the service is about to begin, thrusting a slip of paper into his hand with the words; "Please announce this in the service, pastor". Last minute notices, except in exceptional circumstances, should be politely refused as they can lead to embarrassment. It has to be borne in mind that to announce or publish a notice, implies church support for the content. I remember one occasion when the use of our church premises had been requested by a group promoting a series of lectures on Church History. I announced the meetings and went along myself to the first lecture. To my horror I discovered that the Church History being expounded described all main-line churches and their premises as unworthy of the name of Christ, – and this despite the fact that they were using our premises at the time! Permission for further meetings was immediately withdrawn. This incident is quoted to show how careful one needs to be when accepting and advertising notices, and how necessary it is to find out just what sort of event you will be encouraging.

Handbills, too can be a source of concern. They may again be thrust into your hand as you enter the church building, or someone may be distributing them to your church members as they leave the service. One wants to co-operate with fellow Christians wherever possible but it is wise to check on what is being distributed.

When you have decided which notices shall be announced in church, the next question is 'When?'. I have been in many churches where the notices are given between the reading of Scripture and taking the offering. As the notices are not divinely inspired it is best to finish with them before the lesson is read. In some churches, Notices are given out just before the service. Unfortunately, late-comers miss these announcements.

Many of the problems associated with the 'when', 'what' and 'how' of making announcements are solved by having a printed notice sheet each week that people can take home with them, but this raises the matter of cost. Can the church afford it? It has to be admitted that this does involve expense, but in my experience it is money well spent. Having a news-sheet makes people more aware of what is going on in the church, they feel more involved, and even give more regularly to help maintain the work of the church. Sick and housebound members receiving the news-sheet have a sense of being included in the fellowship. (See Chapter 8 on visiting the sick). It may be possible to offset the cost of production by including a suitable advertisement on the reverse of the sheet, though care needs to be taken to see the ad. does not cause offence. A local press or general store would probably be acceptable, whereas an ad. for wine or tobacco would not.

As well as verbal announcements at the time of worship, notices on a church Notice Board and a weekly news-sheet, some churches produce an occasional magazine which offers even more space for sharing information. A monthly magazine is rather ambitious for most fellowships and a quarterly or seasonal (Christmas, Easter, Monsoon) issue will probably be as much as most can manage. Such a magazine can be very interesting and gives opportunities for young and older people in the church to use their talents to write or report on events. However, production of such a magazine requires a lot of hard work, is time-consuming and can be very frustrating. If the church decides that it would like to have its own magazine, it is essential that an Editor and Sub-Editor should be appointed, perhaps an editorial committee, with the approval of the church committee, to undertake the work involved. While it is advisable, at least in the early days of production, for the pastor to vet the material to be included, it would be unwise for him to accept the responsibility of editorship himself. His role should be that of encourager and adviser. The magazine, marked 'For private circulation only', would contain such items as:

(a) A list of all church activities and their days and times;

(b) A Pastor's Letter;

(c) Names of children dedicated or baptised since the previous issue and persons confirmed, married, and who have died;

(d) Reports on happenings in the pastorate and diocese; Conventions, Youth activities, Visits to Old People's Homes.

(e) Devotional encouragement, Book reviews, Testimonials, Studies.

(f) Humourous anecdotes (cartoons allowed),

(g) Children's page with a short story, puzzle, competition.

Another means of getting news of church activities across to a wider public can be through the media – newspapers, radio and television. Occasionally a radio or television company will want to come and make a recording of an Easter, Christmas or some other special Service. If such a request is made, it is well to make sure ahead of time that the recording crew is instructed in what is and what is not acceptable in a time of Christian worship. It is unlikely that the technicians will be familiar with what goes on in church, and therefore guidance about where they can stand, which parts of the service may be filmed etc., will avoid a great deal of annoyance, both for the camera crew and the church.

Arranging for things to be done 'decently and in order' is not always possible. I well remember one occasion when two TV crews turned up unannounced, each intent on filming our Christmas Day service. The service had just begun when the first crew entered by the main doors, pushed their way through the crowded gathering, shining brilliant lights into the eyes of the congregation. Almost simultaneously, another crew entered the side door and were quite surprised to see they had competition. Taken by surprise, my natural tendency was to cry "Get out!", but remembering in time that this was the season of goodwill and that it would not be to the church's advantage to see its padre featured on the evening news shouting "Get out", I managed to contain myself and suggested to the congregation that they sat down while I negotiated with the television groups to film for five minutes while we would sing carols. Having filmed an unusually self-conscious congregation against the background of the Christmas tree and decorations, the camera crews left, leaving us to pick up the threads of worship.

While this does not strictly belong in a chapter dealing with church notices and publicity, the matter of photography and filming does come up in other connections. These days, couples getting married often want to record the event on video for the benefit of friends and relations. Because of the disturbance often caused, some churches have a very definite rule: "No photography or video recording permitted" and where this rule has been decided upon, then it is necessary to make sure notice of the rule is given when making the wedding arrangements. However, I think that it is possible to include the taking of photographs or video recording without disturbing the sanctity and decorum of the service provided there is careful preparation before the day of the ceremony. The photographers should attend the rehearsal and be shown where they may and may not stand, which parts of the service would be spoilt by flashes, e.g. during prayers and promises, and which sockets can be used for electricity supply. A readiness to co-operate usually brings a co-operative response. None of the churches in which my own children were married allowed photography, but opportunity to pose for photographs was given before and after the actual service and before the couple left for the reception.

As I write the chapter, I realise the printed notice sheets and quarterly magazines and TV cameras may all seem far removed from the village church setting in which many pastors serve. A village community is usually much more closely connected than people living in towns and cities and news travels from one person to another by word of mouth. So they are in the happy position that the problems of communication dealt with in this chapter do not apply in their fellowships.

Committee'd Christians

". . .which is dealt with in Chap 7, part A, Para 3(d) sub-para 1" The Constitution! Most churches have one, and some pay more attention to their Constitution than others. It might surprise some church members to realise that the Constitution is based on Biblical principles and is there as a guide to good organisation and the spiritual welfare of the Church. Misused by unspiritual persons for their own purposes, the Constitution can become a weapon of Satan. Used properly, a Constitution can be a great help in the smooth running of church affairs since it will contain descriptions of the duties of church officers, directions about the frequency and purpose of members' meetings, length of service of elected officers, etc. A pastor needs to thoroughly know his Church's Constitution and each member of the pastorate committee should have a copy, so that proper procedures for the running of the church can be followed and unnecessary disputes avoided.

One thing the Constitution does not stipulate is that the pastor should keep a copy of all letters he sends out, but it is a habit that has developed with me. Possibly failing memory will make it all the more necessary as time goes past, but I have found it wise to make such copies and file them away. From time to time you can have a bonfire of unwanted copies, but there may be occasions when you will be pleased to be able to see exactly what you wrote – and the same applies to Church Notices. Keep a copy of all letters, but filed away, not lying on a table where visitors can read them.

Some churches by tradition allow their pastor a great deal of freedom to make decisions on their behalf. While this may save a lot of time that would otherwise be spent in lengthy committee meetings, it does place a great burden of responsibility upon the pastor who can then be blamed for every unwelcome decision. Sharing power and having written rules is quite Biblical. Ever since Moses was advised by his father-in-law to appoint elders to share his burdens (Exodus 18: 13-26) the concept of shared responsibility has had its place in Biblical thinking. In Acts 15 the Jerusalem Conference gives an example of collective decision-making under the guidance of the Holy Spirit. The decision recorded in verse 29 might be described as an early example of a record of the Minutes! In all our Church Meetings, of the general body or of a Committee, we follow the same principle – that of a number of people coming together to discuss matters of common interest, acknowledging and seeking the guidance of the Holy Spirit in the process of coming to decisions.

When a committee is composed of well-motivated Christians sincerely seeking to do the will of God, then meetings can be times of real spiritual enrichment. Unfortunately, all too often, this is not the case and even well-meaning people manage to get across each other. A pastor may well view the prospect of committee meetings with trepidation because of previous experience of bitter and unchristian attitudes that can be adopted. So how does one prepare for a committee meeting?

Thorough preparation is the key to a good committee meeting. Firstly, spiritual preparation. Time spent in quietness and prayer opening oneself to the ministry of the Holy Spirit will do much more good than time spent in nail-biting anxiety about the issues to be discussed. In this time, the pastor can also prepare a small study from the Scripture with which to open the meeting. The Holy Spirit can use Holy Scripture to point the committee member's minds in the right direction. Then there must be thorough familiarity with the facts, figures and details of the measures upon which decisions will have to be taken. A lot of unnecessary discussion and argument can be avoided and precious time saved, if each member of the committee is also provided with this information ahead of time. It may be helpful, if the pastor takes time to discuss the issues with individual committee members prior to the meeting, helping them to understand the significance of the decisions to be taken, but he must be very careful not to appear to canvas for personal support. Inevitably, the pastor will have his own ideas of what should and should not be done in the life of the church, but he must come to each meeting prepared to listen to all views and humble enough to change his mind, if necessary. He should do everything he can to bring the committee members to a common mind on the matters discussed, and be prepared, if necessary, to postpone decisions to another meeting, rather than force an unwelcome decision upon the meeting.

The chairman (usually the pastor) secretary and treasurer of the church normally constitute the officers of a committee and have a lot of power. To have officers who are united is a blessing, but to have officers who are at loggerheads with each other is a real drag on church affairs. The pastor must work constantly for harmony among the officers. Do not, however, let your efforts for harmony blind you to faults. Sometimes it is healthier to disagree and to postpone a decision rather than try to force through an action that may later lead to dissatisfaction. While working together as a team for the good of the church is to be welcomed, one should avoid giving the appearance of a trio of old school chums just out to support one another whatever the issue involved.

To become a member of the pastorate committee, or any other committee of the church, is usually regarded as an honour. This is fine, provided the person realises that it is an honour that carries obligations. There are numerous tasks to be performed within the life of the church – men's work, women's fellowship, Sunday School, choir, library. . . to name but a few. Not everyone involved in these tasks will be a member of the pastorate committee, but as far as possible, it is wise to see that their needs are represented among the committee members. Those elected to office should know that they are not elected to be merely supervisors but active participants in the activities of the church. A sense of togetherness in service among the committee members, together with the pastor, creates a deeper sense of responsibility and fellowship in the church.

The honour associated with being elected to office can bring a backlash. The elected officer, or even the pastor, may find it difficult to stand down and hand on the job to someone else. In some churches people are still holding office to which they were elected 20 or even 30 years ago when their abilities were most suited to the post. Now, so many years later, to suggest handing over to a younger person and perhaps taking on a new task in which experience and maturity would be more fruitfully used, is resisted at all cost, cost that can be counted in terms of stunted and slowed down church life. A healthy church needs to give opportunity to all members to exercise the gifts given to them by the Holy Spirit and this will involve passing on tasks from one to another as the years pass. How can this be accomplished in a caring way so that no one feels hurt or unappreciated? The best way is to have a definite term of service written into the church rules or constitution. If Mr. A and Mrs. B. know that they have been elected for a definite period of service, then there are no hard feelings when the time comes to stand down and allow someone else to take their place. A system that works most satisfactorily is to have committee members elected for a period of three years, after which they must stand down from the committee for at least one year before being eligible to stand for election again. Not all committee members should stand down each year, then there will be both continuity and change. In small village communities such a system may be unworkable. The thing to ensure is that those normally unheard shall be heard, and to realise that God gives His Spirit and wisdom to ordinary people.

So much for the membership of committees. But what about the matters to be discussed? Questions of finance often affect the items on a pastorate committee's agenda. "Can we afford it?" is frequently asked. In my experience, a healthy church can always afford what the Holy Spirit directs it to do, but this means very careful examination of projects and plans that come before the committee. As elected officers of the church, the members of the church committee have great responsibility for the proper stewardship of the church's money. A wise committee will consider carefully the expected income and probable expenditure of the church and prepare and present a budget to the general meeting of the church body. This allows every church member to appreciate how money is spent, what the financial needs of the church are, what increase in giving will be necessary if new work is to be implemented, and so on. The general body provides guide-lines to the church committee within which they operate. Should a request come for money which falls within the budget guidelines then, if they feel the work is worthwhile, the committee is free to authorise that expense. But should a request be received for a large sum which is outside the limits then it is wise to put the matter before the church body before proceeding with the project. In this way, confidence in the church committee is maintained and doubts about the correct use of church money are avoided.

It is absolutely essential that very correct and up-to-date records of all church monies, however small the amounts, should be kept. I recommend the system of paying ALL monies immediately into the bank without any deductions. For example, Sunday's total collection, having been counted and entered in the church's record, should be paid into the church's bank account as soon as possible. The temptation to take out small amounts for little expenses or the church cleaner's wages will lead to mistakes and muddle. At the time of paying in, a cheque for necessary expenses can be drawn, and the uses for which the money is required can be entered on the cheque stub, which will be a useful reminder for later accounting. Memory plays dangerous tricks on us all, especially in the matter of money, so always record every transaction at the time it is done. A pastor needs to set an example of accuracy in handling church money. If your church has separate funds for different causes,e.g. money for the Bible Society, or Leprosy patients, or if money is held by the Women's Fellowship etc., care must be taken to see that money from each fund is reserved only for the purpose for which it was given. Borrowing from Peter to pay Paul is bad procedure and leads to problems. Some larger churches will find it better to open separate bank accounts for each fund.

Openness regarding all matters of finance is necessary, if the trust of the church is to be retained. So be sure that your committee is fully informed of all financial transactions, and that these have their approval.

Just as finance is a matter that can cause much trouble, so property also can lead to problems. Where there is property there is expense and a need for expertise in maintenance. In some churches there is a Property Committee appointed to look after the property and report to the church committee any work that needs to be done. Such a committee will probably include the officers of the church, but will also have on it men with expertise in property matters – building, costing etc. Members of such a committee with a real love for their church will sometimes do many of the maintenance jobs themselves without payment. This can be a great help to a church and appreciation for such service needs to be voiced. There may be other areas also where the appointment of a sub-committee will save the pastorate committee a tremendous amount of time. The pastorate committee should not hesitate to delegate authority and make use of all the reliable expertise which the membership of the church offers.

Perhaps the meeting that a pastor approaches with the most trepidation is the Annual General Meeting. Often this meeting is more like a display of wrestling where dissidents within the church membership vie with one another. Others may use this as their only opportunity to exercise their speech-making prowess to the utter boredom of the rest of the members. But the A.G.M. should be a time of thanksgiving for all that God has been doing in the fellowship of the church and a time of re-commitment of all the members to service for the coming year. In larger churches members are unaware of what members are doing or of the blessing that various departments in the church have experienced through the past year. Careful, prayerful planning by the pastor and church officers can make all the difference between a miserable meeting and a time of joyful thanks giving and praise. Invite each organization in the church to give a short report, not more than 5 minutes each, of the work that has been going on in the past year, highlighting matters for special praise. Older people are eager to learn of the useful acts of service engaged in by the young people. Young people may be surprised to learn that the men's group has been working in a home for the elderly. Such sharing of information brings a sense of proper pride in one's church. It may even be possible for some of the skills possessed by members to be shown in a display of art or handicrafts. Of course there has to be the business of budget, elections, etc., but people will approach these matters in a more co-operative frame of mind, if the reports have demonstrated the liveliness of the church. The problem of getting a quorum for an annual meeting, which should not be set so high that it is almost unattainable, will be reduced when the A.G.M. is known to be worth attending.

To sum up, the formula of 'Prayer and Preparation' applies equally to the matter of good committee meetings as it does to other areas of the church's life. As a pastor, I can look back on committee meetings that have left me feeling drained and despondent, but I can also remember feelings of buoyancy and thanksgiving at the end of committee meetings when I have felt the presence of the Holy Spirit and a sense of togetherness with God's people in the work of his kingdom. We serve an eternal God who can over-rule our mistakes and weakness, though he asks us to be good stewards and to work to his specifications.

Sharing and Training

Not far from where we live in Britain there are two churches. They are within a stone's throw of each other and both claim to be of the same denomination. Both are finding it difficult to manage financially and in days of escalating costs, it is impossible to have two pastors. Can you guess how these two buildings came to be built in such close proximity? It was because a disagreement in one fellowship led a number of members to separate off and build themselves a separate church. Of those who originated the division, none is alive today and the original cause for separation is probably unknown to most of the present members. Yet, so set in their different ways have these people become, that there seems to be no likelihood of the two fellowships combining again.

Our first reaction to this situation is to judge it a waste of resources and wrong. But who are we to make such a judgement? Only God can do that. It is true that nuances of doctrine greatly affect some people. They cannot find freedom to express worship in situation that they feel do not accord with their own understanding of Scripture or Church government. Others can cope with differences of theology either by ignoring them or by appreciating the aspects of truth in each variant. From a practical point of view, expense and availability of sites may mean that even two churches of different denominations will no longer be able to build separate churches in one new enclave, so one building may have to be used by all Christians in a given area, thus pushing the various Church denominations into new experiments in co-operation.

However, such is life, that a group of Christians may feel led to form a separate fellowship or build a new centre for worship to suit their own inclinations, and how do we feel when such a group opens up shop near to our church? We are disturbed and indignant that our fellowship should be challenged in this way. Certain species of animals and birds have their own territories and will vigorously defend their boundaries against invasion. Vestiges of this territory-consciousness may contribute to our feelings. We feel we have a right of occupation and resent anyone who appears to be moving in. This is understandable and we, as pastors, must look after our own congregations. We have to tend and defend to a certain extent. "Care for the flock in your charge" is a duty laid upon us, not an option about which we can be careless. Yet we need to examine ourselves to see whether this right sort of possessiveness can be exercised in the wrong sort of way. When a garden becomes too large for one person to manage, under-gardeners have to be employed. They have to be trained and they need to know the over-all aims of the owner of the garden. Are we sometimes so possessive about 'our' work, that we are unwilling to allow others to share in it? The outcome of such possessiveness will be seen in the dissatisfaction of members who begin to feel neglected and the weeds will begin to appear in the garden.

A pastor may be put in charge of a particular area – a parish – but he will need to share his responsibilities with others for the good of the whole work. Someone with a gift for organization may not have the gift of relating to children, so part of the pastors work is to discern the gifts of his people and provide opportunities for those gifts to be used and developed. Obviously, the pastor cannot be teaching in Sunday School and at the same time be leading worship in the church, but in sharing responsibility, he must be responsible for ensuring that the over-all aims of the work are being fulfilled. It requires a great deal of patience and humility to work alongside or through some people, but if harmony can be achieved and talents developed, then you will have doubled the output of the church. If however harmony and co-operation are not maintained, then we arrive at the basis for two churches built within a stone's throw of each other – which is where this chapter began.

In chapter 12 reference was made to officers of the church to whom responsibilities are given; the Secretary with his Minutes Book and flair for organization; the Treasurer, with the task of seeing that money is properly accounted for. But there are others with responsibility, e.g. in the Women's Fellowship, Choir, Youth work, Hospitality, Outreach, Mid-week Groups, Nurses' Fellowship, Fabric, Church cleaning, Bible and Book Stall, Church Library, Counselling, Sunday School, Church Magazine, quite a long list. How to keep such a large group with diverse gifts working in harmony? It will largely depend on the pastor. He needs to maintain regular contact with each individual and group serving within the church. Each will face difficulties and problems from time to time, and they need to know that the pastor is there to consult and encourage. While not undermining confidence in their abilities, the pastor can encourage them to take advantage of training schemes, or opportunities to learn from others. It requires a great deal of tact, especially when suggesting to people who have been doing a particular job for a long time, ways of improving the skills which they already have.

A pastor may find it quite easy and satisfying to be an encourager or counsellor for members of his church fulfilling the roles listed above, but what attitude will he adopt regarding Lay leaders or Lay-preachers? So often their contribution falls within the area of the pastor's own ministry; leading worship, leading prayers, reading scripture, preaching, conducting mid-week cottage meetings and Bible studies. If these leaders have attractive personalities, drawing people to themselves in such a way that the pastor begins to feel threatened, is it possible that he will feel jealous and put obstacles in the way of them using their gifts within the fellowship of the church? None of us is above temptation and we need to ask ourselves honestly whether or not we have such a hidden fault. Proper use of the skills and dedication of such helpers enables the church carry out a wider ministry. It may be possible to have an extra mid-week group meeting, or a small 'satellite' congregation in another area of the town where lay-leaders can take respon-sibility for conducting worship. Regular meetings of the pastor with his lay-helpers for prayer and sharing and perhaps, going through the Bible study for the next week's meeting, can lead to a close fellowship of mutual support which the pastor will come to value.

In the chapter dealing with the Call to Ministry, I spoke of the way God leads those whom He is calling, often in stages through Sunday School teaching to Lay-preaching and so on, gradually confirming His call to full-time ministry. It is only by observing people in action and sharing with them in the way I have suggested above, that we are able to give an opinion about their suitability for the ministry, and it is only by taking time to listen to them that we shall understand how God is leading them. Many who read this will recall parents, friends and pastors who in early days gave them encouragement to train for the ministry. We shall be fulfilling our calling as we encourage others.

However true it may be that God gives His gifts, it is also true that those gifts have to be developed. Muscles only develop by exercise. A singer only achieves his best by tireless practice. So also, the person who aspires to lead Bible study will need instruction and opportunity to practice. At first it may be sufficient for the pastor to spend time with the student guiding his reading and discussing his studies, but he will be wise to encourage the student to make use of other helpful courses that are available. TAFTEE Certificate Courses are simple enough for a class VIII student to tackle and at the same time, are deep enough for profitable use by a graduate. Over a period of two years students are led to a thorough grounding in all four Gospels and the Life of Christ. It also touches usefully on Preparing a Bible study, Leading a Service, Relating to people of other religions, Recognising the dangers of occult practices etc. The course is available in at least six regional languages apart from English and can be followed by other courses which include the Ministry of St. Paul and his letters and the Acts of Apostles. Personally, I found my own learning profitably continued through the use of these courses and thoroughly recommend them. Other courses, specially for Lay Leaders may be arranged locally through the denomination. In encouraging those with aptitude to take up these courses, you will be helping them to develop God's gifts, to learn about God's will for their lives and to become more useful and efficient in their service. Your role as pastor is like that of Barnabas. If Barnabas had not encouraged Saul, we would not have half the New Testament, and if he had not encouraged Mark, we would probably have only half of the Gospels! Who knows? You may have the privilege to encourage a disciple like Paul or Mark.

To stimulate interest and whet appetites for more, a church may decide to run its own leadership training course. Interest in Lay Training in my own church grew out of just such a course. It ran one evening a week for eight weeks. Each evening we had three 40 minutes sessions with a break for coffee. The course included introduction to the Old and to the New Testament, Church History, with special reference to how all the denominations of the Church came about and something of their different emphases and traditions, Doctrine and some Comparative Religion. I did not attempt to teach all these courses myself, but drew on the knowledge of others living in the district, including priests from other churches. Among those who took this course, some went on to full time ministry and all were stimulated to study further. Other churches became interested and a Lay Training scheme for the whole diocese was eventually established. Often we hesitate to start something such as lay-training for our members because of a sense of our inadequacy. My advice would be, make a beginning, look around and find what resources there are to help you, and you will be surprised and excited to see how God is at work.

Music in Worship

The first house in which I lived in Bihar was on the banks of the River Ganges in Munger. The centre room of this bungalow was enormous, part of an earlier structure that had survived the earthquake of 1934. Another legacy from the pre-earthquake days was the collection of Christian bhajans composed and set to Indian ragas by John Christian, whose grave is still there in the Mission Compound, and John Parsons. The story goes that to collect authentic tunes, John Christian used to arrange for local dancing girls and musicians from the town to visit his house. Then, suitably hidden behind a curtain, the composer would listen to and write down the rhythms and cadences of the music, to which he would later fit his own words. Bhajans such as:

"Yishu Nam, Yishu Nam," and "Jai jan ranjan," by John Christian & "Jai Prabhu Yishu, Jai Adhiraja," by John Parsons, are still sung enthusiastically in Munger and by other Christian communities. Our hymnbooks contain a great collection of such bhajans and gazals written by men who, like King David, had the gift of composing songs and who were stirred by the divine love of God. Personally, I am not a musician, but if my untrained ear can appreciate the beauty of truth set to music, then surely music can be a channel of blessing to many millions of people. Music is not meant to be used only as a means of entertainment, but can be both a vehicle of praise for worshippers and means of conveying truth to those who want to hear it, as in Sat Sang gatherings.

There is something inherently appealing about bhajans, gazals, zaburs and so on, but it is not only 'religious' music that is uplifting. Good music, both Eastern and Western can convey something of the beauty and wonder of the nature of God Himself. The music played as prelude to worship is meant to bring the worshippers' minds and hearts into a state of quietness when the presence of God can be sensed and His word more readily heard and appreciated. This purpose may be served by using a taped recording of a good choir singing worship songs, or of a piece of classical music.

Let us think about music from three aspects; the use of hymns, bhajans, etc., in regular worship; special services featuring music or musicians; how to introduce new hymns and make the best use of old ones.

Most of us have struggled with choosing hymns for worship. Trying to find hymns which fit the theme of the service can be very time-consuming and often exasperating. Many hymns contain excellent meanings but are spoilt by being in the first person singular; everything is 'I' and 'Me'. This is quite in order for personal devotions, but does not do justice to the gathered Church when we need to be able to sing 'We', 'Us' and 'Our'. Most hymnbooks have the contents divided up into sections such as 'Praise & Worship', 'Holy Scriptures', 'Dedication', etc., and this does help. By using these guidelines we can save ourselves a great deal of time. This may seem very obvious, but the fact is that all too often those leading worship leaf through their hymnbooks, choosing a few well-loved numbers that they think will go well. I found it useful to have my own personal copy of the hymnbook in which I could mark specially appropriate hymns, well-known tunes that went with unfamiliar words, and troublesome hymns – those that contained awkward stanzas or high notes that were unhelpful to the singers or musicians. At the back of the hymnbook, I also kept a list of suitable hymns for funerals which often have to be chosen in a hurry and sung without musical accompaniment, and also a list of Responsive Readings that suited particular seasons or occasions.

Probably you find that because not more than fifty percent of the hymns in the church hymnbook are known by the congregation, your choice is limited. This leads to a repetition of certain hymns. I recall suggesting to an organist that we sing "The Lord's my Shephard" for a certain service, to which she commented, "That's one of your favourites, isn't it?". Without realising it, I had chosen that hymn so often that the organist had assumed it must be one of my favourites! Is there any way we can avoid inflicting the same hymns again and again on our congregations? One way, of course is to have a helpful organist who will remind you of the over-use of a particular hymn. Another effective way is to have a notebook in which the hymns used week by week are recorded. The pages in mine were divided up something like this:

Day/ Date.	H y m n s.				Resp. Read'g	O/T	N/T	Sermon.
Sun. Dec.20								
Xmas Eve.								
25th(1st)								
" (2nd)								
Sun.Dec.27								
Watchnight								

I kept the notebook alongside my copy of the lectionary and Orders of Service booklets, and so could make quick and easy reference to it to see how recently a particular hymn had been used. Once a year I did an 'audit' of hymns. Taking my notebook of hymns, I would make a numerical list of those used during the year, leaving gaps where a hymn had not been used at all. Against each number I made a stroke for every time it had been used. This was quite a revealing exercise that did not take too long. It showed me which hymns had been used over-frequently and pointed out gaps indicating untapped resources.

At one time the choir, organist and I tried to have one new (previously unused) hymn each month. The choir practised it for a couple of weeks before using it. Then one Sunday it would be introduced to the congregation by the choir singing a verse or two before inviting everyone to join in. It was not, however, a routine that could be adhered to very strictly as the need for the choir to prepare for special services, festivals etc., would interrupt the process and the scheme would lapse for a while. However, it was great help to me, to the organist and to the congregation, and it was an encouragement to the choir to know that they were engaged in valuable service.

Anthems and solos are, like everything else, useful on the basis of their helpfulness in worship. A piece sung with clarity and sincerity can be a great blessing, but a soloist who does not hit the right notes or sings flat is not a help and will certainly turn the congregation's thoughts away from worship. The pastor will need a great deal of tact in coping with an enthusiastic soloist whose contribution to the service can only be described as a diversion. Perhaps his or her desire to serve in the church can be directed into an alternative role. On the other hand, professional excellence can also detract from worship when the song draws attention to the singer rather than to God. Such performances have their place and there may be a good use for such talents in other aspects of church life. None of us is without the temptation to personal pride and even the preacher may be in danger of 'performing' each Sunday to an appreciative audience. It is an exercise in humility to make sure that our part in services does not look for personal adulation but in every way exalts God.

Special services, Christmas, Easter, Anniversaries, etc., provide extra opportunities for exploiting the music gifts in your church. But be careful not to overload the service with so many solos and special musical items that it becomes a talent competition and not a service of worship. Occasionally why not have a service of music only, perhaps in memory of a musician or hymn-writer?

Music is a precious gift which can be used in worship and for personal recreation and pleasure, and there are different ways in which the musical talents of church members may be used for the benefit of the fellowship. One of the most enjoyable evenings I remember was a competition for original hymns. Several youth choirs got together and sang songs of their own composing before a panel of judges. Part of the beauty and uniqueness of this occasion was that it was not held inside a church building but had been arranged in a mohalla where mostly non-christian people lived.

A prayer group which met in that area had saved their offerings week by week and had used this money to hire a shamiana with stage, lights and P.A. system, and also for prizes and advertising the event. It was a most enjoyable evening, both in terms of Christian witness and in developing new bhajans. I believe that within our church fellowships there are a number of people with the gift of writing lyrics or composing hymns and bhajans. An occasion like that described above, or a qawali evening or mushaira, provides the opportunity for talents to be brought out into the open that might otherwise remain hidden and become lost to the church.

We need to preserve the heritage of music that comes to us from the past. There are and always will be changes in styles of music, and our young people especially like to keep up-to-date with new songs and rhythms, and that is to be encouraged. At the same time, it will be a great loss to the Christian community, if compositions of 50 or 100 years ago are not preserved and occasionally taken out for an airing. In these days of electronic recordings as well as printed hymn books, there are those among us who can act as librarians to preserve the store of music and words handed down to us. Older persons in the Church should be encouraged to record these before they are forgotten.

Chapter

15

Disputes and Problems

The pastor may be the last person to learn of trouble brewing. For him the first indications may be when he notices gaps appearing in the subscriptions book or previously regular attenders fail to turn up at meetings. It may even be that an anonymous letter appears in his morning mail, or a handbill with scurrilous information about one or more of the church members, claiming to have been written by 'well wishers' or 'Your fellow members' – usually unnamed, or even worse wrongly named. Apart from an initial reaction of utter disgust, how does one deal with such matters, and indeed, with all disputes that sadly flare up in church fellowship? The trouble with troubles is that they often do not have one simple origin but are a mixture with various threads and many roots.

A quick look at the phenomena may suggest that quarrelsomeness is the price of Protestantism or of Non-Conformist ideology. But this is not the case. Resentments, injustices, discrimination, self-centredness bubble up in all denominations and can take various forms. It is worthwhile reflecting on three passages of Scripture:

i) Jesus Himself said, "Stumbling blocks are sure to come.

. . ." (Luke 17: 1-4) indicating that the presence of the Kingdom of God does not mean complete absence of disturbances.

ii) He told the parables of the Wheat and Tares (Matt. 13:30) and the Sheep and Goats (Matt. 25:31f) where even the 'goats' address their Judge as 'Lord'!

iii) The parable of the netted fish (Matt. 13:47-50) where both good and bad are netted by the spread of the Kingdom, and a sorting out takes place after.

There is no escaping the fact that Tares look every much the same as Wheat, and all sorts of fish get swept into the same net. Only God and His angels can sort them out in the final analysis.

There is potential for good and bad within all people, so it is important for us as pastors to recognise that we ourselves are not perfect. Our parishioners may call us 'Father' out of love and respect, but we are capable of a sad distortion of the Fatherliness of God Himself (Matt. 28:8-12). We need to admit our failures to ourselves and to God, and sometimes to others. If we have spoken slightingly of a person, or offended a person, then we must admit it and ask for forgiveness. To stand repentant and forgiven in Christ is our hope of final righteousness. It is only as we live repentantly toward God and are daily dependent upon His forgiveness that we are able to bring others to this same experience. As leaders we are called upon to make judgements, but never to be judgmental. We so easily see the speck in our brother's eye, be that a brother placed above us, beside us, or one in our charge, but find it difficult to recognise our own faults. The Holy Spirit can point out our failings to us, and sometimes chooses to do that through a fellow human being, – and how unwelcome this can be! It is a humbling experience to be told of our failings by another, but even if it is not done in love, accept it in love. Welcome the criticism, and take the opportunity to put right the offence.

To keep on ministering to God's people in the power of the Spirit, while at the same time needing His ministry ourselves is a wonderful discipline. The 'feed my sheep' passage of John 21 was not put there for Peter's comfort. It is there to illustrate that a truly repentant person can still be used by Christ as an under-shepherd. Where the gospel is preached, there has always been opposition. It happened in the days when Jesus was on earth. It can be expected these days also. In fact we should be uncomfortable, if we find life too comfortable! Disputes throw us off course, diverting energy of mind, body and spirit, away from God's work into quarrelling. It is playing the Devil's game to give all our attention to the dispute. This is not to say that quarrelling is harmless. Where truth is twisted and the Church is rendered impotent by divisions, we detect the work of the deceiver. Evil seeks to take advantage of all disputes.

Yet out of wrong disputes good can sometimes come! One of the worst times I experienced in the course of my ministry was when a dispute in the church lasted over many months. With hindsight, I can see where my mistakes may have contributed to the problem, but I can say that I did not seek or desire such a dispute in any way. It was a most unpleasant experience, yet the amazing thing was that out of that time three good things happened. First, a number of people in the church realised in a new way just how damaging such quarrels are to the life of the church, and they began to meet together for special times of prayer. The intercessory ministry of this group was not only a very strong factor in the eventual ending of the quarrel, but led on to a continuing ministry of prayer within the church. Secondly, a Christian evangelist involved in the ministry of healing visited our town in this period. His meetings were well attended and some of our people were led to form a regular prayer-for-healing group within the church. The needs of those in ill health were regularly brought before God, and sometimes members of the group went out to pray with and minster to sick people. The group continued on long after the dispute became history. Also interest in the work of the Friends Missionary Prayer Bands started and the church decided to support a missionary couple both in prayer and financially. It seemed amazing to me that so much good could be emerging during a time of upset and turmoil, but this was a lesson I had to learn.

Problems arise, and they will not go away by being ignored but rather grow worse. You will have to tackle problems. Here are a few simple points, easily said but not so simple to apply. They come out of personal experience and so are commended:

1. Prayer. Personal prayer at regular intervals keeps us in touch with God's resources and saves us from relying entirely upon our own wisdom. Having prayed, leave it to God for a while!

2. Self-examination. Ask yourself: 'Has there been any way in which I have by omission or commission contributed to the problem? Is there something for which I should ask forgiveness?'.

3. Where possible, get the prayer support of others, possibly a prayer group, or fellow minsters (who may or may not be of your own denomination) or close associates.

4. Consider enlisting the help of a wise third party to act as mediator. This may be especially appropriate when you yourself are involved in the dispute.

5. Use hospitality. Many misunderstandings can be put right, around a meal table.

6. Use speech. Talk to those concerned, not about them to others.

7. Use persistence. Don't expect everything to clear up at your first intervention. Persist in showing love to all concerned. Even when there has been reconciliation, harsh and unkind words and attitudes are not easily forgotten, so your perseverance in love will bring its reward.

8. Rely on God to be at work as well! God will be using other means as well as your ministry to prepare His people for reconciliation. It may be through words they hear on a Christian radio programme, or through their own daily Scripture readings. Your own sermons, though they must never be written with a particular person in mind in order to point out his error, may still, in the normal course of following the lectionary, contain just the word that enables a quarrel to be brought to an end. The Holy Spirit uses more ways than we know to reach the depths of people's hearts, but this does not excuse us from doing our part also.

9. Always be ready to forgive.

10. Finally, don't let problems dictate the programme for Church life and ministry. Because your thoughts will constantly return to the problem, make sure you allow God's word to direct the aims of your ministry.

Some pastors are posted to serve congregations where there is a long history of hostility. Families line up against each other. Maybe the pastor is resented and complaints flow thick and fast. How can you minister against such an unpleasant and joyless background? Remember, you are still the pastor. You still have to present the gospel. If you have to point out a flagrant sin, do so as quietly as possible. We have to follow Christ's example in not ignoring sin, yet always seek to reclaim the transgressor. People may try to ruin your reputation and this is extremely hurtful, but hold on to God. Let the Holy Spirit minister to you. Be faithful and know that the Truth has its own power to convict of wrong and lead to repentance.

Chapter

16

A Pastor is Always Learning

Whether Film Star, Prime Minister or Priest, perhaps only his family know just how human is the man some set upon a pedestal. The ethical perfection found in Jesus Christ lays down a standard to which we aspire, but of which all of us constantly fall short. Even our non-christian friends are able to point out where we and our community fall short of the ideal. Some of us may be Bachelors of Divinity, but none of us is a master of divinity! If a lay person engages in some sort of shady deal, somehow it doesn't register as high on the religious "Richter" scale as when a pastor is caught out. Acknowledging our humanity, we are sometimes overwhelmed by the high standard required of us. When Jesus said, "Be ye perfect." (Matt. 5:48)persumably this was meant for all His disciples and not just for the apostles. Christ was the image of the invisible God, made perfect. . . without sin. We have a Leader and Lord worthy of honour, an exalted calling, a privileged heritage, The service of Christ is a marvellous and joyful involvement, so let us enjoy it!

But who among us would not admit to tensions and failures? We who should be leaders find ourselves surpassed by others. We who should be full of faith find ourselves timidly doubting, weak in the very matters in which we are supposed to help others. First, we have to realise how human we are. Our bodies, intricately constructed, impose limitations upon us. They need a rest now and again. They need refuelling and maintenance. Most people need a good night's rest and can be irritable if they do not get it! We need to eat at fairly regular intervals and we need relaxation and exercise. This applies to all people including church members and pastors. We may think that our failures stem from some spiritual lack, but it may be that we are pushing our physical strength beyond a wise limit, or we may not have a good diet.

Many who are in deep trouble come to us and unburden themselves. We know the problems and sufferings some of our people have to bear. It is small wonder that we also find ourselves oppressed by these burdens. Early in my ministry a senior colleague advised me, "Stand back from the problems other people have and do not get too emotionally involved." At the time I did not appreciate what he meant. Of course we have to be involved! We are told to "bear one another's burden" – that is part of Christian discipleship. Yes, it is! Yet I can see now that to serve these very people best, I have to remain slightly aloof. After all, a doctor does not serve his patient best by getting into a hospital bed with him!

Although we hesitate to talk about it, one cause for anxiety for many pastors is their comparatively poor salary scales. This is true not only of India, but also of Africa, South America and even parts of Europe. In India, where wandering sadhus are supposed to have renounced all attachment to material possessions, or Buddhist monks are seen with their collecting bowls, perhaps the idea that a religious person needs an adequate wage is regarded as novel. Pastors accept that theirs is not a profession where financial rewards are great. However, many of the financial needs of churches and pastors could be adequately met, if Christians tithed their incomes. I think that many church members would be encouraged to do just this, if they were confident of careful stewardship and management of all the church's finances. Openness and accountability in all matters concerning money enables members to give to their church funds with confidence.

It is also true that the tent-making ministry is not extinct and perhaps, for some pastors and churches, this may be the way forward. For a pastor to have a salaried secular job alongside his pastoral duties calls for understanding and adjustments from both church and pastor. There are dangers that need to be recognised. The pastor may feel himself to be so independent that he does not co-operate well with either his church committee or with his denominational authorities. The church may feel that they no longer need pay any of his expenses, not even those directly relating to his ministry, and this can lead to tensions. Understanding and co-operation are needed, if this type of ministry is to succeed. My own experience has been that, though there have been times of difficulty, God has never failed to supply my needs and I am glad to have been able to give my full time to the pastoral ministry.

Looking back over many years, what lessons suggest themselves? Let me attempt a list:

1. Regular Bible study provides a guide for one's personal decisions as well as being a constant source of material for preaching and teaching.

2. Visiting members in their homes is essential for understanding and maintaining good relationships. I would give this high priority on the list of pastoral duties.

3. It is worth having a time-table for each day, even if again and again it is interrupted.

4. People need and appreciate Bible teaching.

5. Most church members, even when in disagreement with the pastor, are willing to be guided by the Bible.

6. Lay Training courses, whether a small project within one's own church fellowship, or linked with other churches or the diocese, have been most beneficial.

7. The more you put into the ministry the greater satisfaction you get.

8. God supports those who rely upon Him. Worldly wealth does not guarantee contentment.

9. To learn to rebuke that which is wrong in a loving way is very difficult, but necessary.

10. A pastor is not exempt from Christian disciplines. For example, he does not have the right to teach about timing, if he himself does not practice it. He cannot ask his members to add several hours a week to the hours they spend at their secular jobs in order to serve the church, if he himself is not giving at least the same number of hours to his pastoral work.

11. Never presume you are too strong to be tempted or to fall.

12. Never neglect the ministry of prayer for all your members. Regular prayer for each member should go alongside regular visiting.

The list could go on, but I hope that in sharing some of the lessons I have learned in my years in the ministry, I have also been able to share the sense of privilege and joy that the work has brought. Ours is a high calling for which only the Holy Spirit can equip us. My prayer for you all is that you may experience the joy of Christ's blessing on your ministry.

-o-o-o-